A REGAL BIBLE COMMENTARY FOR LAYMEN

GOD'S WAY OUT

Finding the Road to Personal Freedom Through Exodus

BERNARD L. RAMM

Regal Books
A Division of G...
Ventura, Ca...

Published by Regal Books
A Division of GL Publications
Ventura, California 93006
Printed in U.S.A.

Originally published under the title *His Way Out.*

Library of Congress Cataloging-in-Publication Data

Ramm, Bernard L., 1916-
God's way out.

Rev. ed. of: His way out. 1974.
Bibliography: p.
1. Bible. O.T. Exodus—Criticism, interpretation, etc. I. Ramm, Bernard L., 1916- . His way out. II. Title.
BS1245.2.R35 1987 222'.1207 87-12872
ISBN 0-8307-1215-1

1 2 3 4 5 6 7 8 9 10 / 91 90 89 88 87

Contents

A complete Leader's Manual for Bible study groups using this course is available from your church supplier.

Introduction to
Exodus

The Stature of the Book

Exodus is a tremendous book. Writing this commentary on it has required living with the book hour after hour, day after day. Studying Exodus carefully, watching the plot unfold, one is conscious of its impact. The book has an inner momentum and a logic that the reader feels moving through its pages. There is grandeur in its themes and a marvelous doctrine of God—certainly one of the greatest in all of Scripture.

Exodus sets out the basic theology of holy Scripture. Granted that certain great seed doctrines appear in Genesis, and that Exodus has no doctrine of creation comparable to that in the book of Genesis, but on all other points, the fundamental theology of holy Scripture is set forth in Exodus.

Let us look briefly at some of these great theological themes:

Exodus is *the book of divine redemption.* It tells how an enslaved people gain their deliverance from the "iron-smelting furnace" (Deut. 4:20). Deliverance from Pharaoh becomes the motif and typology of all deliverance in Scripture. Deliverance from one's enemies becomes the background for understanding deliverance from one's sins.

The *doctrine of sacrifice* begins with the passover lamb in chapter 12, the sealing of the covenant in chapter 24, and the consecration of the priests in chapter 29. There are sacrifices in Genesis, but the theology of sacrifice begins in Exodus.

A *theology of worship* begins in Exodus. The Tabernacle is the unique structure for the worship of God. It is perpetuated in the Temple and becomes the basis of expressions in the New Testament for the worship of God.

The great *foundation of biblical ethics* is laid in Exodus. In addition to the famous Ten Commandments there are the ordinances of chapters 21—23 that have found their way into so much common law in the West.

The *calling of the prophet* begins with Moses. Abraham was called a prophet in the sense of a powerful intercessor before God (see Gen. 20:7), but the unique role of a prophet as a man of the Word of God surfaces with Moses. As a leader, Moses anticipates the judges, the kings, and then the Messiah (see Hebrews 3).

Moses is the theologian of the Old Testament. He received specific revelations of the nature of God, especially in Exodus 3, 33 and 34, but the knowledge of God is implicit in the whole record. For example, the desire to redeem Israel implies the great love of God; the law implies the justice and holiness of God.

The book of Exodus *introduces the priesthood.* The complementary New Testament book of Hebrews is rich in drawing out the priestly ministry of Christ as foreshadowed in Exodus.

Finally, the *theology of the covenant,* which is so prominent in holy Scripture, receives detailed treatment in Exodus. In Hebrews 9 and 10 the author wishes to show how great the new covenant is in Christ, so he singles out the giving of the covenant in Exodus 24 from all the Old Testament covenants as the most significant.

The Name of the Book

The Hebrews named the first five books of the Bible (*Pentateuch*—"five rolls") by the first word or two. Exodus is called, "And these are the names," or simply "names" (*shemoth*).

When the Hebrew Bible was translated into Greek (the *Septuagint*) in the third century before Christ, new names were given to the books of the Pentateuch. *Shemoth* was called *Exodos.* This is from two Greek words—*ek,* meaning "out of" and *hodos,* meaning "road" or "way," hence "the way out," "the escape," or "the exit." In classical Greek it meant a marching out of an army, the going forth of an army to meet the enemy, a solemn procession, the piece of music played as someone made an exit, the mouth of a river, or one's death as an exit from life.

It was renamed *Exodus* in the Latin translation (the Vulgate), from which it comes into the English Bible.

The Interpretation

This book is more of a running commentary on Exodus than a strict verse-by-verse commentary. We will deal with a Hebrew word or a point of grammar only if something important is at stake. Our emphasis is on: (a) God—His attributes and activity; (b) types and shadows of Christ and His church; (c) prophesy which bridges Exodus to the New Testament and (d) the spiritual meaning and practical application of Exodus to our lives.

In the last case, we are imparting some meaning into the text, because we consider this book part of the Word of God to the Christian church. To note facts of grammatical, historical and geographical significance and remain totally silent about the possible spiritual meaning is certainly not to write a Christian commentary. It may be academic and historical, but the church lives on the Word of God, not on the academic and historical (but not in violation of the academic, historical and grammatical).

The New Testament has many references to Exodus and many allusions to its contents. We therefore feel that on New Testament grounds we have the right to bring New Testament truth back to the book of Exodus. Not to do this would be contrary to the great Reformation principle that *Scripture interprets Scripture.* The context of Exodus is the entire Scripture!

How Israel Understood Her History

In order to understand Exodus and the use of Exodus in the rest of Scripture, we must understand Israel's concept of history. Israel understood her history in three unique categories:

The principle of representation. The Hebrews held that the great events of Exodus belong to all the generations of Israel. All future generations share in the historical events of Exodus. Hence, these events must be represented. Basically they are represented through annual festivals. Such festivals are the New Year, the Day of Atonement, the Passover, the Feast of Unleavened Bread and the Feast of Tabernacles. In each of these festivals, some aspect of the Exodus is enacted. As it is enacted, the event is represented.

The principle of participation. When the event is represented, subsequent generations participate in the meaning of those events. In modern psychological language they "identify" with those events. This first is an act of

faith. The subsequent generations believe t
events happened; they believe in their significance; and
they accept their significance as valid for them. This
means that a purely historical view of Exodus is inadequate.

The principle of enlargement. Exodus is in small what world redemption is in large. Pharaoh in small is in large all of God's enemies. Israel in small is in large all of God's redeemed people. The Passover lamb in small is the great atonement of Christ at the cross. To go over and over a great event in the history of Israel and give it ever-increasing meaning is typical of the way in which the prophets treat the Old Testament history and the New Testament treats the entire Old Testament.

This is one of the principles that support our right to read theology backwards into Exodus. Nehemiah 9 and Psalm 78 are lengthy recitations of the Exodus experience. If such a procedure has biblical warrant, why should not Christians see their typology in Exodus?

Historical and Geographical Setting

The book of Exodus claims to narrate events that took place in Egypt and the Sinaitic Peninsula. The time period is that of two Pharaohs. When we read the book as history, as we understand history today, it seems to lack a great deal—but certain things need to be said.

These events took place about three thousand years ago. Dates and places are, therefore, not easily ascertained. We can judge from remarks about the age of Moses and other chronological remarks that most of Exodus is limited to a forty-year period. We can even shrink that down. From the time Moses returns to Egypt and leads the Israelites out to Sinai and completes the Tabernacle, we have a period of something like thirteen months.

Egypt and the Sinaitic Peninsula have been scoured in the attempt to locate all geographical references. Some identifications seem accurate; others are educated guesses. However, the main line of Israel's route seems certain. The Israelites started eastward from Egypt, turned south, crossed the Red Sea and headed along the southwestern part of the Sinaitic Peninsula. Then they cut southeast to the mountains at the end of the peninsula, where the best location of Mount Sinai is.

The important matter to the author of the book is the events and their meanings; matters of history and geography are secondary. But he is not opaque to the need for such references and he adds them when they are important. But this means that, from the standpoint of scientific history and scientific geography, much is lacking. The fact should not surprise us.

Any schematized book will have similar lacks. Exodus is a highly schematized book in its story of escape from Pharaoh, the receiving of the Law, and the building of the Tabernacle. But historians have the right to schematize. We must, therefore, expect no more from Exodus than it intends to deliver, as fascinated as we are in our times by accurate historical materials and geographical references.

How to Use This Book

The presupposition of the exposition that follows is that the reader has read the corresponding text in Exodus before looking at this book. It is hoped that he or she has read it many times and in different translations.

Further, it is expected that the reader will have the Scripture open to the passage being discussed so that his eye can skip back and forth from commentary to Bible.

1
Toughing Out the Tough Times
Exodus 1:1-22

Divine Redemption

Exodus 1—8 tells the story of Israel's escape from forced slavery in Egypt and of the beginnings of the wilderness wanderings—from the land of Goshen to Mount Sinai. The Exodus is alternately called *Salvation and Redemption.* The Greek word *exodos* can mean "an escape." Exodus tells how Israel escaped from Egypt by God's help and power.

The human instrument God used for this escape was Moses. Moses was God's spokesman to Israel, as well as Israel's leader, organizer, judge and teacher. As leader of Israel he was her king; as the man of the Word of God to Israel he was her prophet; and as the one who interceded for her that she should not be destroyed, he was her priest.

In accordance with the entire teaching of holy Scripture, we must see the narrative operating on two levels. On the first level it is the record of how the descendants of Abraham, enslaved in Egypt, escape their bondage and become a free people and a holy nation.

At the second level, it is the typology of all deliverance in Scripture. Phrases taken directly from Exodus or derived from Exodus are scattered throughout the Scriptures. Pharaoh, his people and Egypt itself stand for any and all powers, visible and invisible, that oppress man. Moses as the deliverer stands for all of God's deliverers and for deliverance.

Accordingly, the New Testament calls Christ the Second Moses (see Heb. 3:5,6). He is also called our Passover (see 1 Cor. 5:7). Further, Paul draws a parallel between the Israelites in Egypt eating the passover meal and the Christians and their eating of the Passover (see 1 Cor. 5:8).

Redemption is the basis of all biblical religion. Redemption without sacrifice, a mediator and mediation is unknown to holy Scripture. The great typology of redemption set out in Exodus is fully realized in the person and work of Jesus Christ who founds the new Israel of God (see Gal. 6:16).

This story of redemption begins with Israel enslaved in Egypt.

Free Israel Forced into Slavery—Exodus 1:1-14

According to the account of Joseph in Genesis, Israel was once a welcome guest in Egypt. Jacob and his sons came to Egypt as free men and equals with the Egyptians, for Joseph's wisdom had saved Egypt from seven terrible years of famine.

Then comes the tragic line: "Then a new king [or dynasty], who did not know about Joseph, came to power in Egypt" (1:8). This Pharaoh[1] could have known the name of Joseph, but that is not the burden of the verb "know." He did not know the significance of Joseph, nor comprehend that through Joseph's wise planning Egypt had been rescued from mass starvation. Had Pharaoh known this, he never would have forced Joseph's descendants into slavery. Certainly sin is more than ignorance; however, ignorance may be a fertile field in which sin may grow. So it was with Pharaoh. And so it is with all who are ignorant of God, His ways, His Word and His Son.

A king's fear that a group within his kingdom may rise up against him has many parallels in the ancient world. The territory where Israel was, was especially vulnerable to warring tribes and attacks from the west and northwest. Some have estimated that counting all the foreign population in Egypt, one out of three inhabitants at that time could have been non-Egyptian. If this was the case, then the sudden growth in the number of Israelites would have been highly distressing.

Pharaoh's method of coping with the problem was inherently evil. The rest of the record depends on this assumption. The Israelites had come to Egypt at the invitation of Joseph and his grateful Pharaoh. They had come as welcome guests because of Pharaoh's indebtedness to Joseph. The Israelites were not Pharaoh's property nor possession. How cruel and unjust to submit the sons of their deliverer (Joseph) to slavery. This, too, was a custom of old-world kings.

Such slavery achieved two things. It reduced the possibility of war, and it gave Pharaoh a great source of labor. The text says that the Israelites were "worked ruthlessly" (v. 13), that their lives were "bitter with hard labor" (v. 14) and that they were treated with terrible severity. They did construction work ("brick and mortar") and bone-wearying agricultural work ("all kinds of work in the fields").

This slavery did not catch God asleep any more than anything in this world does. In the revelation of His purposes to Abraham, He had told Abraham that his descendants would be oppressed as slaves in a strange country (see Gen. 15:13). God works in the pushes and pulls of history, even though we who live in the midst of history and cannot see the end from the beginning often have no way of detecting His work. But faith believes He is there! In Egypt! At the cross! In our lives! In the history of our world in our times!

A Desperate Pharaoh and Faithful Midwives—Exodus 1:15-22

As verses 13 and 14 reveal, Israel's slavery was bitter. It was to be even more grinding. The more the Hebrews[2] were oppressed, the more they multiplied. The more they multiplied, the more they were dreaded (v. 12). Now the fat was in the fire. Pharaoh had broken the centuries of peace and became the persecutor of Israel. There had to be an outcome, a victor in the struggle. Slavery had provoked the visible Hebrews and their invisible God.

Seeing that slavery itself did not solve his problem, Pharaoh stepped up the pressure by asking two midwives ("Beauty" and "Splendor" were their names in Hebrew) to kill every Hebrew baby that was male.[3] Little did Pharaoh know that the God of these midwives was to give as one of His most fundamental laws, "You shall not murder" (Exod. 20:13). Now to bitter slavery Pharaoh added death. As though in reply, the tenth plague was also to be a death, but a more painful one: the death of the firstborn.

Little did Pharaoh know what he had started, nor the

dread outcome. However, he did force an issue for the midwives. As daughters of Israel, they certainly felt that killing male babies was wrong. Yet they were under the command of the king to do so. They had to choose among their fears: (a) to fear the invisible God, or (b) to fear the visible Pharaoh with the visible signs of his power—his soldiers and his jails. Faith sees the *real* power; sight sees the *immediate* power. Sight fears Pharaoh; faith fears God. The midwives feared God (v. 21).

The lesson here for Christians is obvious, but the execution of the lesson in concrete terms of life is always difficult. To walk by faith is to see the invisible God against the visibility of the world, to trust the Word of God over against the concrete pictures of our senses.

Pharaoh detected that the male children were not being slain, for the Hebrew population continued to increase. The midwives said that the hard-working Israelite women were too fast in delivering their babies. Delivery was so fast that members of the family witnessed a birth before the midwives could be summoned, and in such situations the babies could not be killed. There was partial truth in what they said; how much was falsification the record does not affirm.

God rewarded the midwives with families or large households. Here, as in Job 42, the reward was immediate and tangible in terms of what the midwives could understand and enjoy. A future reward of eternity, rather than time, is a concept long in developing, for man finds it so much more difficult to grasp.

Twice Pharaoh had been thwarted. He could no longer leave the dread job of killing the male infants to the midwives. He now commissioned "all his people" (v. 22) to kill the male children. No wonder the future judgment of the plagues was so severe. No longer was it solely the work of Pharaoh to make life bitter for Israel. Now the whole population joined in.

The necessity for an exodus is becoming clearer. God could not allow the Israelites, as free heirs of Abraham, to remain slaves in Egypt, with their offspring subject to the cruel hands of any man.

Notes

1. The word *Pharaoh* comes from the Egyptian "Big House." Hence it meant the ruler or king in the Big House. "Pharaoh" is a transliteration, not a translation.

2. The term *Hebrew* is a special one for Israel during the period of the Pentateuch. The words *hapiru* and *habiru* appear in ancient inscriptions. At first scholars thought that both words were related to *Hebrew.* This is not the case, but it appears that the *hapiru* were a class of immigrants settling in a foreign nation and that Israel in Egypt belonged to this class.

Israel (the name of Jacob, the father of the founders of the twelve tribes) is the most customary name for the Hebrews in the Old Testament.

Jew is derived from *Judah* and is a much later exilic name for the Hebrews.

3. There is no agreement about the two stones (v. 16, translated "birthstool"). They apparently were a bench or seat of some kind used in delivering children. An interpretation that is a little remote but not totally beyond consideration is that it meant that the midwives were to look at the sexual organs of the baby to determine whether or not it was a male.

2

God Can Use Even You!

Exodus 2:1—4:17

The Providential Deliverance of the Deliverer—Exodus 2:1-10

The whole story of Israel's sojourn, captivity, and return to Palestine was foretold to Abraham (see Gen. 15:12-16). We should expect, then, providential acts of God throughout Exodus as He fulfills His promises, and so we find especially in this passage. The Israelites were confused by their unexpected slavery; but it was within God's providence so that they might learn, as we all must learn, that God delivers us not so much out of life's hardships as through them.

In His providence God used one fact that Pharaoh did not count on: the heart of a woman can be swiftly melted by a baby. Even people who hate one another still love the others' babies and toddlers. God used the compassion of a woman for a baby to save His deliverer.

Moses'[1] mother is Jochebed and his father is Amram (see Exod. 6:20; Num. 26:59). She was a brave woman to save her child, an intelligent woman to devise a plan to save her child. Above all, she was a woman of faith, so much so that she and her husband made the Honor Roll of Faith in Hebrews 11:23.

So far the heroes of Exodus are women!

The mother knew that the river flowed by the king's palace and the place where the royal daughter bathed. (The Nile was considered an emanation of the god Osiris and therefore its waters were believed to have magical properties.) Pharaoh's daughter recognized the child as Hebrew. Would she kill it? No, the crying child aroused her pity and she disobeyed her father the king. Again it was a woman who was the instrument of divine providence. At a dimension Pharaoh never suspected, he was outwitted by the all-caring God of the slaves!

Even more, the child was returned to his mother for his nursing and upbringing. Before he received a line of Egyptian training he was educated in the history of his own people. He learned of the patriarchs and the great covenantal promises made to them. When he became a man and had to make a decision concerning which heritage he should own up to, there was no question. He was true to the people and religion of his mother.

When he was of age he was adopted by the daughter of Pharaoh ("and he became her son," 2:10). This means that Moses became her legal son and heir. In addition to those things he had learned from his parents, Moses received an Egyptian education.

There has been much speculation about the nature of this education. Some scholars have attempted to recreate from data available the kind of education Moses would have had. Stephen says that "Moses was educated in all the wisdom of the Egyptians and was powerful in speech and action" (Acts 7:22). Others have noted how much superstition, etc., were part of the "educated" man's training in Egypt. Nevertheless, in the royal household he must have learned a great number of things of great use later on.[2]

What quietly pulses through so much of this record is the remarkable providence of God. At every turn little events—or big ones!—forwarded the purposes of God in Israel and thwarted the evil intention of the Pharaoh. Yet how unaware were the actors of the providence that guided them all.

Christians who are aware of God's acts in history should always have a firm faith in the overarching providence of God. We should also be reticent to label as "of the Lord" too quickly, for we are just as ignorant of the course of providence while in its midst as were the Israelites and the Egyptians. Silence before the providence of God takes more faith than a ready labeling of events as "of the Lord."

The Right Man, the Right Mission, The Wrong Way—Exodus 2:11-15

The record does not tell us where, but somewhere Moses got the notion that he was the man to deliver Israel from her oppression. Stephen says that Moses was forty years old when this happened and that Moses presumed that God was delivering the Israelites by his hands (see Acts 7:23-25). This section does reveal that Moses knew that he was a Hebrew, that the Hebrews had been wrongfully made slaves, and that he was Israel's deliverer. He also surmised that his brethren understood that God had appointed him deliverer.

Hebrews 11:24-26 makes this a great decision of faith by Moses: "By faith Moses, when he had grown up, refused to be known as the son of Pharaoh's daughter. He chose to be mistreated along with the people of God than to enjoy the pleasures of sin for a short time. He regarded disgrace for the sake of Christ as of greater value than the treasures of Egypt, because he was looking ahead to his reward."

This means that at age forty Moses renounced his rights as the son of the royal daughter. How he considered this a decision for the Messiah we are not told. But it does reveal a very high sense of the meaning of God's stake in the history of Israel.

Moses went out to "his own people" (2:11). The teaching of his parents had gotten through. He knew where his real identity was. He looked at the burdens of his people with a burden on his own heart. The beating of a Hebrew by an Egyptian revealed part of the daily life of the Hebrews. It must have been a severe beating, for Moses killed the Egyptian.

The next day he witnessed another exchange of blows, only this time between two Hebrews. Although Moses thought that nobody had seen him kill the Egyptian and hide his body in the sand, the Hebrews knew! They presumed that a man violent enough to kill another man, even an Egyptian, could well kill them. So they denied Moses the status of a ruler and a judge over them (both words express the right to hold court, judge and assess penalties).

Moses correctly guessed that if the Hebrews knew of the murder, Pharaoh would also know. Pharaoh could not let a murder of one of his people by a Hebrew go unpunished. So Pharaoh ordered Moses arrested for the crime. In the meantime Moses fled to Midian.

Moses' mistake is not hard for us to decipher from our perspective. From Exodus 3 we learn that he was God's chosen deliverer. It was wrong that the Egyptian beat the Hebrew. But murder of Egyptians one by one would never redeem Israel. There Moses was wrong. God would give

Israel deliverance by the hand of Moses metaphorically—not literally! God's will must be done God's way.

Is not this a lesson we all need? Fanaticism in religion is acting without first making a rational assessment of our action! It is foolishness to presume that what is right in our eyes is God's will.

Education in the Ways of the Desert—Exodus 2:15-22

Before Moses could be the deliverer, ruler and leader of his people, he needed two kinds of education. He needed forty years in the Big House of Pharaoh to learn how to organize and manage people, to master the administration of law, and the crafts, art, skills and techniques of a highly civilized people. He also needed to know the rough ways of a semiarid country, for he would spend forty years in such terrain with Israel. So now he fled to Midian where he would complete his education.

The implication of the text is that his flight was providential. He escaped Pharaoh's soldiers in the nick of time (2:15). However, he still bore his Egyptian identity—whether in clothing, accent or in general contrast of a "city" man with "country" people—for the Midianites[3] called him an Egyptian (v. 19).

We see the physical virility of Moses. He had strength enough to kill an Egyptian; to make a trip to Midian; and to fight off the shepherds. No time element is specified in the text, but Moses spent around forty years in Midian, so we do not know how soon after his flight the episode at the well took place.

Had Moses given up his mission to deliver Israel? The fact that he married, settled down, became a shepherd (3:1) and started to raise a family suggests as much. Naming his first son Gershom, which implies a transplanted person or an alien without rights, may indicate his state of mind. If Moses had become dispirited and had lost his sense of mission to Israel we can better understand the call he received at the burning bush.

If our interpretation is right Moses received his B.A. in political administration in the household of Pharaoh and his M.A. in desert survival in Midian. He was now educated for the great mission of his life.

The history of the success of Christianity has been the history of gifted and/or educated people. Paul was the leading rabbinical student of his time. Augustine has been called the most learned man in the Roman Empire of his day. Luther, Calvin and the other Reformers were almost all "university men," trained in the scholarship of Renaissance humanism. Certainly God can use anyone. The history recorded in Judges is proof of that. But other things being equal, we serve God best when we are prepared. It took eighty years to educate Moses! This should cause us to think twice before we belittle a sound education.

Besides gifts, God's grace is also revealed in Moses. Moses was a murderer. He slew the Egyptian without due process of law. As terrible as Moses' sin was, it did not put him out of the purposes of God. In His grace God would still use this man. This is no softening of the Scripture's hard line against sin. It is a reminder that if God used only perfect or spotless vessels there would be none to use. Grace can forgive, cleanse and renew a murderer for the service of God.

Unfortunately the church has made a catalog of nice sins and bad sins. "Nice sinners" can be forgiven and allowed to serve in the church; "bad sinners" are forgiven in word but not in heart and spirit and they may not occupy important places in the church. Moralistic, legalistic Christians always stumble over the depths of the grace of God.

Covenant Promises Are Never Forgiven—Exodus 2:23-25

The story of Moses' call or recall for his mission is preceded by three verses packed solidly with meaning. They present the lamentable state of Israel and the mercy and faithfulness of God.

The phrase "that long period" (2:23) suggests many years of slavery. Then the hoped-for event occurred: the Pharaoh died. But there was no change in policy. The oppression continued. So great was the slavery that Israel groaned under its burdens and cried in prayer to God. These are all very strong words indicating the depth of suffering and despair and revealing that their hope was not in the death of a Pharaoh but in their God.

"Their cry for help because of their slavery went up to God" (v. 23). It came to the throne of grace—a far more powerful throne than that of Pharaoh! The text uses four verbs to record the depth of God's response to the groanings and the cry: God heard . . . God remembered . . . God saw . . . God was concerned!

God is not unaware of human sufferings and wretched human predicaments. When God is silent man concludes that He is ignorant of human conditions or indifferent to them. It strikes the sensitive conscience as cruel if God is either ignorant or indifferent. However, God had His time schedule.

God's schedule for the Exodus required that two conditions be fulfilled before He would move: (a) Moses had to learn the ways of the desert so that he would be an effective leader; (b) the Pharaoh who sought his life had to die so that Moses could return to Egypt in safety. These two conditions had now come to pass and God was ready to act.

How or why did He act? First, on the basis of the suffering of Israel. God does respond to human misery. But equally so in this case God responded because of His covenantal promises made to Abraham: God "remembered his covenant" (v. 24).

A covenant is a unique Old Testament concept. It is not exactly a contract although it has similarities to one. The word for "covenant" and "will" are the same in Greek (*diatheke,* whereas contract is *syntheke*). A will is made by a man exercising his personal sovereignty over an estate; it need not follow strict lines of equity. So a covenant is made by God exercising His royal sovereignty.

God makes a covenant not only as sovereign Lord but also as gracious Lord. He is not driving for terms, negotiating a settlement nor haggling over a contract. He graciously proposes the terms of the covenant to man and pledges His infallible word to it. The passage of time, no matter how great, does not invalidate the covenant. God's Abrahamic covenant was still in effect with the children of Abraham in Egypt!

The God of Jesus Christ is related to Christians personally and covenantally. A personal relationship hangs gingerly on the quality of the relationship. A breakdown in the quality of the relationship may end the friendship. In contrast, a covenantal relationship is according to God's grace and specified terms. God responded to Israel's misery, but also to His covenant. Hence a covenantal-personal relationship is the strongest possible relationship and Christians are bound to God the Father personally and covenantally.

The covenantal dimension insures us of God's grace. It is God's grace that sustains the covenant, not man's spiritual strength or goodness. Because it is not based on man's fidelity or ability to perform, it gives a stability not present in purely personal relationships. Christian stability is grounded in the stability of the covenant we have in Christ. God hears our prayers not only on the grounds of our misery, suffering and groaning but also on the grounds of the New Covenant in Christ.

The Deliverer Is Uniquely Called—Exodus 3:1-6

We have noted that Moses apparently had had some sort of call to be the deliverer of Israel. His murder of the Egyptian, his flight to Midian, his married life and his work as a shepherd seemed to have either dimmed or effaced that call. A new, clear call was needed and Moses received this call in chapter 3.

The call came in a place where there was feed for the flocks and at a place known for some kind of divine manifestations, for it was called "the mountain of God" (v. 1).

Many times Moses had built a fire while tending the flock. Such fires were necessary for warmth, for cooking and perhaps to frighten off wild animals. But wood in such a country was scarce as it still is in the Middle East.

When Moses saw "flames of fire from within a bush" (v. 2) he was seeing something very much within the boundaries of his own experience. Yet for wood to oxidize and not turn to ashes was unusual. This would be even more marked in the case of a frail bush that would ordinarily be burnt up in a few minutes. Moses, therefore, paused to inspect this phenomenon. God had caught his attention!

God called Moses by name out of the burning bush (v.

4). That God calls people by name is one of the most reassuring facts of biblical revelation. It speaks of the intensely personal character of God's dealings with us.

There is a pile-up of deity in this short passage. First God's presence is signalized by the angel of the Lord (v. 2); then we have the name of Yahweh, then Elohim in verse 4; followed by "the God of your father, the God of Abraham, the God of Isaac and the God of Jacob" (v. 6). Moses needed to know who was speaking to him out of this bush far away from Palestine where Abraham lived and far away from Egypt where the children of God now were. This was the God of the covenant of 2:24! This was the God who remembered and would now act!

The Advent of God into Egypt—Exodus 3:7-12

God was moving! Notice the strong verbs: "I have indeed seen . . . have heard . . . am concerned . . . have come down to rescue them . . . and to bring them up . . . am sending you . . . will be with you . . . have sent you." The promises of four centuries standing were about to be realized!

The most compelling of all the expressions is "I have come down" (v. 8). It is a common Hebrew verb for God's participation in man's history, but the spatial metaphor is interesting. God is in heaven and man is on earth. In heaven God *knows* the condition of Israel, but only as He comes down to earth can He *redeem* Israel.

The Christian thinks of John 1:14, "The Word [came down to earth and] became flesh." God loves man from all eternity. From His heavenly throne He knows man's terrible plight. But love and redemption become actualities only in the great act of condescension and humiliation of the Incarnation. As God came down into Egypt to redeem Israel, so Christ came down into the world to redeem man.

The basic biblical and New Testament pattern is set out in the text. It is *from* Egypt and *into* Palestine. It is from the "iron-smelting furnace" (Deut. 4:20) into a "land flowing with milk and honey" (Exod. 3:8).[4] Redemption is *from* a state of bondage *into* a state of freedom. Romans 6 is a beautiful commentary on this fact. In union with Christ in His death we are redeemed *from* the law of sin and death. In union with Him in His resurrection we are redeemed *into* the life of those who live as though they had risen from the dead. We must not only exult in our great redemption from the consequences of our sinful life, but also rejoice in the great salvation and everlasting life into which we have been delivered. Negation of sin must yield to affirmation of new life in Christ or the gospel becomes pure escapism.

This commission, "I am sending you," was a problem to Moses. The first time he attempted to rescue Israel he blew it. At Horeb God told him to go back to Egypt to confront Pharaoh and to bring "my people the Israelites out of Egypt" (Exod. 3:10). How could one shepherd with only a staff in his hand challenge the whole court of Pharaoh? So Moses ducked out with a rhetorical question: "Who am I"? (v. 11).

God's reply was: "I will be with you." The strength of God would prove greater than the weakness of Moses. Although Moses blew it the first time, God's wisdom would guide him in the right decision this time. Further, Pharaoh, the Egyptians and the Egyptian army could not match El Shaddai—God Almighty! No general nor adventurer nor explorer ever started with better equipment and assurances than Moses did with the promise of God to be with him.

The Christian mind turns to a similar situation when the risen Christ commissioned a handful of Jewish common folk to evangelize an entire world! He said to them words very similar to those spoken to Moses: "Surely I will be with you always, to the very end of the age" (Matt. 28:20).

Further, a sign was given Moses. He would later worship God in this same mountain of Horeb. Note that there was no immediate sign. This was a "historical sign." The most durable proof of the reality of God and His work in our world is the witness of the divine presence in the unfolding of the years, decades, centuries and millennia. In this sense the greatest proof for the reality of God is history.

The Great Name of God—Exodus 3:13-22

As a good Semite Moses asked what he should say when the Israelites would inquire for the name of God. The name of God would identify the God who made such a promise and it would suggest that He could keep the promise. To a Semite a name meant the personality, character or nature of the inner reality of whoever was being named. To ask for the name of God was to ask for the nature of God in its most profound aspect.

God said that His name is "I am who I am" (v. 14) or "I will be what I will be".[5] The name, which means "I am the One with you," indicated how the God who made such an unimaginable promise could be relied on to keep that promise. It suggests that the promise will be kept because God is always with Israel as He promised to be with Moses (v. 12).

There is a future thrust in the core verb used here. It suggests such variations as "I will be continuously with you as future events unfold," "I am a God who participates in your history so that as events come I am in them," or "I am the living, acting, ruling, participating God, in this world, so I will be with Israel in the events of her redemption."

As we have suggested only in the course of historical events can God really be known. This is the way we know people. First impressions may be way off target. The longer we know a person and the more experiences we go through with him the better we know him. The purpose of courtship is to determine whether the first impression of attraction to another person is worthy of a more permanent relationship than friendship. It would be the experiences of the ten plagues, the destruction of Pharaoh's army in the sea and the providence of God in the Wilderness of Sin that would reveal the name of God.

The elders of Israel (v. 16) were the leaders of the tribes of Israel. These people would hear and believe the promise of the Lord. Moses was not quite sure of this point.

"A three-day journey" (v. 18) was some sort of common expression but we are uncertain of its meaning. Such retreats for the worship of one's God were customary in that world. Three days may mean a typical period for such a retreat. It may mean "not too far away so don't worry," or just the opposite, that a substantial distance was to be put between Israel and Pharaoh.

In verses 19 and 20 we first surmise the extent of the struggle that would precede Israel's release. Pharaoh had to be compelled by a mighty hand (v. 19) before he released Israel. The "mighty hand" is an anthropomorphism (i.e., speaking of God in terms of man) for the great power of God. The "mighty hand" of God would bring to pass ten plagues here called "wonders" (v. 20) because of their power to reveal the presence of God. Then Pharaoh would release Israel.

The deeper motifs or themes of the Exodus were now being built up. It was to be a great contest between the Lord and Pharaoh, the Egyptians and the gods of Egypt. In this struggle we see that redemption was a contest that emerged into victory. The Lord of the slaves would triumph over the gods of Egypt. This great struggle and the deliverance became a type, a model and an example of all deliverances of God in both Testaments.

The Israelites were not to leave Egypt empty-handed but to ask for jewels and clothing and to put these on their children (vv. 21-22). Some commentators consider this action unethical and most deal extensively with this problem.

First, they uniformly reject the idea of borrowing. The word used is a strong word for asking and not merely borrowing.

Second, some commentators affirm that the jewelry and clothing were the wages of slavery. According to later Jewish law (see Deut. 15:13,14), Israel had served the proper time of a slave and more. After that time had elapsed they deserved wages and this is how they received them.

Third, the demand could be taken as part of the humiliation of the Egyptians. The Israelite children wearing the precious jewels and clothing of the proud and mighty Egyptians would suggest the reversal of their roles. The slaves were free!

Fourth, the event could be regarded as providential

since later in their history Israel would build the Tabernacle and would need all the precious metal they could get.

God's Prophet Needs God's Credentials—Exodus 4:1-8

The Scriptures are more realistic about the problem of revelation and faith than moderns give them credit for. Today it is presumed that if a man has a religious faith he has lost his powers of separating fact and fiction, reality and fantasy. According to Freud, religion is a useful, psychological illusion, but there is no spiritual world. Many moderns agree with Freud.

Moses knew that he could not appear before the elders of Israel and brashly confront them with the incredible promise of God to deliver them. They would presume that God had not talked with Moses but that Moses had had a talk with himself—a soliloquy! They would say: "The Lord did not appear to you" (4:1). Faith does reduce to credulity if it does not find something objective "out there," in reality, in the course of events, to substantiate it as defensible action.

God gave Moses three signs with which to reply to the elders if they denied that the Lord had spoken to him. All of these signs were "in-the-culture" signs. They were signs that Israelites and Egyptians of that culture would understand. They would show the Israelites three things.

First, they would show that Moses was not inferior to the magicians of Pharaoh's court; second, they would show that Moses had the same (and greater) powers as the Egyptian magicians; third, they would show how superior Moses was because he could take a snake by the tail and not the neck and still live. As far as can be ascertained the snake would have been a cobra.

The snake was a symbol of royal and divine power of the Pharaoh and was on his diadem. Moses' feat then was more than paralyzing a snake by bending its head back so it was like a stick and then tossing it on the ground and breaking the spell. It was aimed at suggesting that the power of God was greater than Pharaoh's.

Leprosy and other skin diseases were a common curse of that old world. Today we know how magnificently complex the skin is and how many diseases afflict it. To cause and cure one of their dreaded skin diseases was then truly a sign of God's power.

Finally, the river Nile was divine in the mind of the Egyptians. To turn it into blood was a further sign of the greatness of the Lord over the deities of Egypt.

The problem of the miracle, sign and wonder that runs through the whole record can be discussed at this point. The views expressed among the commentators can be stated as four different opinions:

1. These stories are Jewish elaborations of some obscure events or pure elaborations. Such fairy stories never really happened.

2. They are pure miracles. Any drawing on so-called natural factors to explain them undermines their supernatural origin.

3. For the most part they represent some sort of conjunction of divine power and natural phenomena associated with the land of Egypt. *This is our stance.*

4. God was in these events but the original event has been obscured. Moses may have caught a skin disease and been cured of it, but the time element is so condensed that it appears a sudden cure. Or these miracles are "miracles of coincidence." Nothing supernatural in itself happened.

The miracles were natural events or phenomena that did occur in Egypt. Yet their occurrence was so timed with events in the life of Moses and Israel that they cannot be denied as providential. God was truly, historically at work at this level but not in the obvious supernatural way Christians have generally understood the accounts.

The first position is ruled out as contrary to Christian faith as we understand it. It is simply a capitulation to the modern post-enlightenment mentality presenting itself as scientific, or factually oriented or freed from mythological ways of understanding reality. It is really a victim of its own mythology.

The second position is ruled out because it is so evident in the text that that which is happening is a mixture of the natural and the supernatural.

The fourth position is ruled out on the basis that it is another version of "the king is naked." If all the apparently supernatural is reduced entirely to the "miracle of coincidence" then the unbeliever will reply: "Just as I thought; nothing of divine causation happened out there in space-time-matter reality. It is all in your head. This is so typical of you religious people. You confuse the musings or fantasies of your own mind with reality." So pretended scientific respectability or academic integrity is purchased at the price of being unable to affirm before a hardheaded, historically-skeptical and empirically-oriented audience that God truly does come into our space and time and make a measurable difference.

A Great Insight into the Nature of Divine Revelation—Exodus 4:10-17

From Moses' complaint that Israel would not listen and believe (silenced by the promise of the three signs) he moved on to the complaint that he was not eloquent. The Lord replied by stating that He made man's mouth, He made people deaf or blind (v. 11). Could He not activate the tongue?

Two things may be said here: (a) This passage does not affirm that all who are so stricken are smitten of God. Rather it means that if God wills He can affect the organs of man. Therefore if He wills He can make Moses' tongue eloquent. (b) The Hebrews had no concept of secondary causes such as a specific organism (a virus or bacteria) that could cause blindness or deafness but attributed all that happened to God, the Creator of all. Thus they considered the Lord to be the Author of all the conditions that produce blindness or deafness. This view might be a welcome theological addition to our way of looking at things, correcting an excessively scientific and cause-oriented way of regarding our history and cosmos.

Still Moses did not respond. What was holding this man back? Was it fear? But fear of what? Pharaoh? The Egyptians? The Hebrews? Himself? The text does not say, but it was a paralyzing fear of great magnitude. He asked that somebody else speak for him. In anger God said that He would send Aaron with him (v. 14).

Can God get angry? Yes, the text says so!

One of the debated problems among theologians today is whether God sits in His heaven, immovable and impassible (i.e., incapable of suffering), perfect and self-contained or whether He suffers when we suffer. It must be the latter; but our belief in His sharing of our sorrows must not detract from the importance of the perfection of God. Our actions and reactions do get through to God. He is a Father who pities His children. We have a great High Priest who can be touched (i.e., moved) by our plight (see

Heb. 2:17-18; 4:14-16). If God can love, if God can repent, if God can be jealous, then God can be reached by our predicaments.

Of course, God does not experience things as we do. He suffers but never with our kind of distress. The course of history may sadden or gladden Him but it can never surprise Him. His disappointments are relative, not absolute and shattering as they may be with human beings. This concept may cause problems for man but not for holy Scripture: Scripture abounds in both affirmations of the perfection and infinity of God and declarations that God loves, repents, hates and is jealous as He views human history and the human race. He is not an Aristotelian God lost in His reflection, not caring for man.

In Exodus 4:16 God tells Moses that when Aaron speaks for him he shall be to Aaron as God. This is a remarkable assertion. It reveals in part the process of divine revelation. God will be with the mouth of Moses so that Moses will speak God's Word; Aaron will hear the Word from Moses and speak it to the Israelites and Egyptians. Aaron can only speak what Moses says, and only Aaron will speak what Moses says. As the mouthpiece of Moses, Aaron is acting as if Moses were God to him. Revelation is God speaking through the mouth of one man to another. To take all of this painfully literally is to miss the kind of communication that takes place.

Revelation starts from point *A* (God); it proceeds to point *B* (the prophet); he in turn speaks it to point *C*, his fellow man (Israel); and it may be, if God so wills, it moves to point *D* to be cast in written form (Scripture). So here in passing we have a great insight into the nature of revelation.

It was the same with our Lord. Many times in John's

Gospel, especially in chapter 17, Christ says that He speaks the Word or the words of God. From point *A* (the Father), we have the divine Word coming to point *B* (the Son), who is heard at point *C* (John) and is written in a book at point *D* (John's Gospel).

This section clearly reveals God's determination to use Moses—in spite of his faults, weakness and resistance—to accomplish great things in His name. Take heart, struggling Christian. The powerful, loving God of Moses can also use you!

Notes

1. Most scholars believe that the name of Moses is a play on words in which Moses means one drawn from the water. In Egyptian *moshe* means "name." Cassuto thinks that this is wrong. An Egyptian gave Moses his name and it is some variant of "son" and only reminded the Israelites of the verb *Masha,* which means "to draw from the water." Cassuto thinks *Moshe* is closer to the Egyptian or Hebrew word for deliverer (*Commentary on the Book of Exodus,* pp. 20,21).

2. While the majority of scholars accept the documentary view of the origin of the Pentateuch and reject the idea that it is a composition of Moses, many of them believe that a man of Moses' stature is behind the record. R.F. Johnson writes: "The link between Moses and Israel's emergence from Egypt is such an intimate one in the biblical narrative that it seems almost impossible to question its authenticity" (*Interpreter's Dictionary of the Bible,* K-Q, p. 441). Our most recent and most thorough discussion of Moses to date is Dewey Beegle's *Moses, The Servant of Yahweh,* in which the author asserts that despite critical problems one cannot doubt that such a historical person as Moses is behind the record (p. 30).

3. The Midianites were descendants of Abraham through his concubine Keturah and her son Midian. Hence, they were distant relatives of the Hebrews. They were desert-dwellers, living east of the Jordan and Dead Sea and south down to the Gulf of Aqaba. The book of Exodus does not mention a possible language problem of a Hebrew coming to Egypt and conversing with the Egyptians, nor how Moses could talk with Midianites. However, if present analogy means anything, people piled on top of each other (e.g., Switzerland, Lebanon) will easily acquire two or more languages, and in other parts of the world there are "trade languages."

4. The land flowing with milk and honey is Palestine. Palestine is derived from Philistia or Philistines, the ancient foe of Israel who lived on the plains of

the coast and were famous for growing wheat. It is also called the land of Canaan because of its occupation by the Canaanites. It is called the Promised Land because it is promised to Israel in view of the Abrahamic covenant and because it stands for a condition of Israel so different from the bondage of Egypt (cf. Num. 14:30, Deut. 9:28, 19:8 and so on). The title "Holy Land" is Christian and originated during the Middle Ages. However, compare Zech. 2:12.

5. The God whose name is "I am that I am" (introduced as Elohim) is also identified as "the Lord" and "the God of your fathers." The purpose was to be sure there was no mix-up. The God with this unique name was still the God of Abraham and of the covenant.

"LORD" is the older name of Jehovah. Jehovah is derived from the four Hebrew consonants, YHWH. Originally Hebrew was written only with consonants called radicals or roots of words. The vowels were added later. The Jews believed the name too sacred to pronounce. So they took the vowels from another name of God, Adonai, and inserted them in YHWH, hence Jehovah. Modern scholars believe that the correct vowels produce the name YAHWEH.

3
Getting on with God's Program
Exodus 4:18—7:7

Moses Puts Feet to His Faith—Exodus 4:18-23

All Moses' objections had been cared for by the Lord. Moses accepted the divine commission and set out for Egypt with his wife and children. Naturally he had to obtain permission from Jethro, who released him. Furthermore God assured him that those who had sought his life were dead. Fear for his life may have been the cause of Moses' extreme reluctance to return to Egypt.

What a great portent is in the words, "And he took the staff of God in his hand" (4:20). By the power of that rod Pharaoh and the Egyptians would be humiliated, the Red Sea would open and close and Israel would receive providential care in the Wilderness of Sin.

What a marvelous title Israel is given: "my firstborn son" (v. 22). In that ancient world the firstborn son was the most cherished of children. He was the principal heir of the father and carried on the family tradition, name and possessions. Hence we see the severity promised against Egypt: If the Egyptians did not let Israel go, they would suffer the loss of their firstborn sons. Calling Israel God's firstborn son is using a warm, intimate, family expression to suggest the closeness in which Israel stood to God because of His covenant with them.

This closeness is also a theme of the New Testament. One of the dearest names for Christians is sons of God, indicating the special family-like relationship they sustain to God the Father (see Heb. 2:10; 12:7,8; 1 John 3:1,2; Rom. 8:14-17,19; Phil. 2:15).

With verse 21, this section introduces the theme of the hardening of Pharaoh's heart, so we will discuss it at this point and let it cover other instances that occur later.

To modern man, God hardening Pharaoh's heart sounds like a primitive view of an autocratic God. Maybe it made sense in a civilization where a king's word was the law and never to be challenged, no matter how arbitrary or cruel. However, modern man cannot accept such an unethical concept of the rule of God. Is this the case?

Under pressure, commentators have attempted to relieve this pressure by different formulations:

1. The hardening of Pharaoh's heart is another example of the Hebrew view of causation. Secondary or intermediate causes are eliminated and causation is affirmed to be immediately of God. Retranslated into our language it states that "the circumstances of the plagues hardened Pharaoh's heart."

2. God *occasions* the heart of Pharaoh to harden, but does not *cause* it to harden. This is like saying "the circumstances hardened Pharaoh's heart."

3. It is said many times that Pharaoh hardened his own heart. This clearly reveals that it was a circumstantial hardening, and not God's judicial hardening.

4. Nowhere is it said that Pharaoh's eternal salvation

or status before God is involved. The hardening of his heart is purely instrumental in revealing the power and glory of God (see Rom. 9:17).

There is merit in each of these four assertions that we do not deny. However, we believe none of them gets to the root of the matter as Paul does in Romans 9. The theme in Romans 9 is that the terms by which God and man are related are stipulated by God, not by man. Mercy and judgment are God's prerogatives. Man cannot compel God to act a certain way nor demand that God act a certain way. Man can respond only to the conditions set out by God. To think otherwise is to destroy the Creator-creature relationship, i.e., the vessel would be dictating terms to the divine Potter (see Rom. 9:19-23).

Man in his sinful pride wants to control his own religious life and expects God to conform. He thinks that by setting out his own terms, he is preserving the ethical relationship between himself and God. He wants God to respect his efforts to be moral and religious. He is saying in so many words, "Dear God, please reward me for my moral and religious life as you are a God who wishes man to be moral and spiritual."

In Romans 9, Paul sees it very differently and for good reason. To base man's relationship to God on man's moral and religious accomplishments is to rely on a rope of sand. Therefore God takes this responsibility away from man and keeps it for Himself: "It does not, therefore, depend on man's desire or effort, but on God's mercy . . . . Therefore God has mercy on whom he wants to have mercy, and he hardens whom he wants to harden" (Rom. 9:16,18).

This means that God sets the terms of the divine-human relationship. It is God who sets the terms of salvation (showing mercy) and judgment (hardening the heart).

But this is no divine determinism. It is a relationship of grace. It means that man's hope for eternal life rests upon God's grace and fidelity and not upon the frail arm of man. If God is not the Rock of our salvation, then we must despair. If we think that we save ourselves by manipulating God, by forcing Him to respect our morality and religious life, what an impossible thing we ask. We are flesh! Our lives are like vapor that disappears in a few moments! We need the divine Potter! We need the covenant-keeping God! Then there is hope.

But grace and wrath go together in Scripture. If God is sovereign Lord in grace, He is sovereign Lord in wrath. One cannot talk about grace in salvation and speak entirely of human doings in wrath. The God who saves is also the God who hardens. If we remove hardening from God, we must also cast loose from sovereign grace! But there is one difference. God rejoices in His grace. There is a tragic side to hardening. Hence Paul writes that God endures with much patience those whom He hardens (see Rom. 9:22,23). No, God has no pleasure in the death of the wicked! Grace and wrath exist together in God, otherwise we have hopelessly sentimentalized our view of Him and lost His character as holy love. But God's joys and triumphs are those of grace and not of wrath. Wrath is always God's second choice.

That God could harden Pharaoh's heart is also the hope of Pharaoh. For the God who can sovereignly harden can also by His sovereign grace melt and win to faith.

A Man of the Covenant Must Keep the Covenantal Terms—Exodus 4:24-26

In Genesis 17:9-14, circumcision is made the sign of the Abrahamic covenant. The uncircumcised male who violates the covenant is to be cut off from the people of the covenant. On the surface, it seems that Moses in Midian with a Midianite wife did not circumcise his son. As a man of the covenant he could scarcely return to Egypt to the Israelites with an uncircumcised son. The man of the covenant must keep the terms of the covenant.

Some commentators consider Exodus 4:24-26 the oldest in Scripture and loaded with obscure references. They see it as a very old story in which a desert demon seeks to kill Moses (or whoever the original person was) and is thwarted by a magical rite of circumcision. The obscurity of the passage is brought to light in reading what the earliest rabbis said about it. It was as difficult to them as it is to us.

Some Jewish commentators take the passage in the best possible light. It is a passage that shows the importance of circumcision in the Jewish culture. Whether it was a circumcision of Moses' son, or a vicarious circumcision of Moses (for Exodus nowhere records his circumcision), the point is that circumcision was a major part of the Abrahamic covenant and Moses had neglected to keep it. He could not return to Egypt and Israel without setting this matter right.

Seeking to kill Moses means that Moses came down with a serious illness; if it had not been averted he would have died. He apparently knew why. "So the LORD let him alone" (v. 26) means that the sickness abated and Moses recovered. Being so sick, he could not circumcise himself (if it were a vicarious circumcision), nor his son (if he had neglected his circumcision in Midian). A flint knife was used as it was considered a sacred material, whereas a metal knife would defile. Most commentators take feet to be a euphemism for Moses' sexual organs.

Once again, no matter how obscure the passage is, what is not obscure is its meaning. It means that the leader of Israel could not lead Israel until he had meticulously kept every detail of the Abrahamic covenant. Otherwise he could be charged as a covenant-breaker and lose his hold on the Israelites.

God Was Right, Moses Was Wrong—Exodus 4:27-31

God sent Aaron to meet Moses at the mountain of God and to return with him to Egypt (4:27-31). Aaron would be Moses' mouthpiece and would speak the good news to Israel.

Moses' great fear was that the Israelites would not believe the wonderful news he would bring. God assured him that they would. When Aaron told the elders the good news and Moses performed the signs, the people did believe! Even more, "they bowed down and worshiped" (v. 31).

They had forgotten or forgiven the man who murdered an Egyptian in a misguided effort to save Israel. They had kept the faith of the patriarchs, for they not only believed the renewal of the patriarchal promises, but they worshiped. Decades of hard slavery had not drilled that out of them. God will always have His people on this earth. Neither apostasy nor heresy nor persecution can efface His people. The miracle of preaching is that *some* will believe—not all, but *some!*

We must not be too optimistic about these people. Later on they would turn to murmuring, then to idolatry. Christian experience is also such a "mixed bag." We are all children of dust and never too many paces away from error, weakness and sin.

The First Try to Release Israel Backfires—Exodus 5:1-23

If Moses thought that he was to announce that Pharaoh should release the Israelites and that Pharaoh would immediately consent, he had not listened carefully to what the Lord had told him. The Lord had warned him that it would be a stiff contest and that only under maximum pressure (the death of the firstborn son) would Pharaoh release Israel.

When Moses and Aaron announced their claim to Pharaoh he replied with a surly, "Who is the LORD, that I should obey him . . . ? I do not know the LORD" (v. 2). How true and how tragic! Why should a king who considered himself among the gods have respected the God of people that were slaves? If only he had known the Lord! If only he had known that He was Creator of heaven and earth! If only he had known the history of Joseph! If only he had known the plagues that were coming! If only he had known the drama that would soon take place at the Red Sea! If only he had known that all the earth belonged to the God of Moses (see Exod. 19:5)! If only he had known, he would have spared himself and the Egyptians some terrible experiences and let Israel go.

Is it any different today? Men do not really know the God and Father of our Lord Jesus Christ. Men do not really know of the Incarnation, the Cross and the Resurrection. If they did they would bow their heads and worship Father, Son and Holy Spirit.

Pharaoh's response was to make slavery more bitter, bondage heavier and tasks more difficult. He sent out new instructions to his foremen: (a) the slaves must collect their own straw, with no lessening of the number of bricks to be made; (b) heavier work was to be laid on them; (c) the Israelite foremen were to be beaten; and (d) the request to go three days and worship God was to be considered dishonest and an excuse for idleness.

Bricks were made by mixing mud and straw. It made a durable brick, for some of the Egyptian brickwork may still be seen today. The Israelites had to scurry all over Egypt to find straw and still produce the same quota of bricks each day (v. 12).

The foremen of the Israelites complained to Pharaoh that his new demands were unreasonable. Pharaoh's reply was, "Lazy, that's what you are—lazy!" (v. 17). Here is the master-slave relationship at its worst. The slave complains that he is overworked; the master claims that the slave is lazy. However, we can guess some of the arrangement of Egypt of that time. The Israelites were organized with foremen of their own over them, and these foremen did have access to Pharaoh.

When they left Pharaoh's Big House, the foremen encountered Aaron and Moses. They accused Moses of making them "a stench" to the Egyptians (v. 21). Further they complained that by asking for the release of Israel, Aaron and Moses had "put a sword in their hand to kill us" (v. 21).

Moses was confounded. With all the promises and assurances of God, he did not expect things to backfire this way. Instead of Israel being released, her slavery had become unbearable. So he prayed to God and told Him that instead of delivering His people He had only done evil to this people (v. 22). Why such a discrepancy between what God had promised and what was actually happening?

The mistake of the foremen and Moses was that they presumed how God would work. They thought that one word to Pharaoh would cause him to release Israel.

Because He didn't work the way they anticipated, they were offended. Granted it would have taken great faith to see God working through the increased pressure of their slavery and the greater hostility of Pharaoh; still, a great faith would have believed that.

Christians, too, may be plunged into spiritual uncertainty if they "program" God. We ask for spiritual distress if we imagine how God will act in a certain situation. Faith would have seen that Pharaoh was screwing the lid down hard, only to have it blow up higher. So we should have great patience in the hard rows of life when we think God is absent. We never know what greater blessings will come out of those times.

God Is Not Sitting on His Hands—Exodus 6:1-9

God hears and answers prayer even if it is the complaint of a confused man! Printed prayers may have their place in a liturgy. There are times of urgency, however, when the heartache of man can be expressed only in spontaneous prayer. So it was with Moses. His prayer did not ride on beauty of language but on the cry of his heart. At the opening of chapter 6, God answered Moses' prayer by saying in so many words, "I am not sitting on my hands as it appears to you and the elders of Israel. I will act!"

"I am the LORD" (v. 2) is a typical expression in the proclamation of a king. It means that a royal edict is now coming. And so it did here. God was about to fulfill His promise and carry out His purposes. This is the burden of the verses that follow.

In verse 3, God says that He was not known by the name of "the LORD" (Yahweh) to Abraham, Isaac and Jacob, but only by the name of "God Almighty" (El Shaddai). The patriarchs knew the name in a purely rational sense, but not in a profound sense. Israel could know the Lord in the deeper meaning of Yahweh only through the exodus experience. God is going into action and He is going into action not as El Shaddai, but in order to reveal the real meaning of Yahweh.

"Now you will see" (v. 1) suggests that God had been waiting for this moment. Neither Moses nor the foremen of Israel could know under what conditions God would move. That time had now come. Yahweh would now show what *Yahweh* meant. It meant that God is the God of action, of power and of compassion for Israel.

In this hour of increased oppression, God renewed His pledges to Moses and gave him several encouragements: (a) "I am the LORD" (v. 2) means "I am the kind of God who can take sovereign and effectual action. Conditions could and would be changed!" (b) Because the Abrahamic covenant is "established" by God (v. 4), it was still in force and God would now keep its terms. (c) God had heard the groaning of the Israelites (v. 5), which means that He was moved not only by the covenant but also by man's wretched condition. There is the tender expression "I will take you as my own people" in verse 7. If Pharaoh had only known their true identity in God's sight! (d) God would redeem His people. The word "redeem" in verse 6 refers to a member of a family buying back or ransoming another member of the family, especially when that member was in slavery for debt or about to go into slavery. Israel apparently had no earthly relative to redeem her, but God was now Israel's relative, her kinsman redeemer. (e) This redemption was to be not only out of Egypt but into the Promised Land.

The Israelites heard all of these words but could not

believe them. Their "discouragement and cruel bondage" (v. 9) stifled any faith in their hearts. Faith would have seen through the cruelty of Pharaoh to the surety of God's words. But we must not blame these Israelites. Suffering can be so intense for a Christian that he or she may be unable to embrace the sure promises of the New Testament.

Regardless of the failure of Israel to respond, we have a marvelous group of promises in these verses. How clearly they reflect the great things done for us by the God and Father of our Lord Jesus Christ! It may be said that the Old Testament saints did not know the meaning of *Father.* The great compassion of God in Jesus Christ as revealed in the New Testament provides us with the riches of the concept of God as our heavenly Father. Not in nature and not in philosophy of religion but only in redemption through the divine Incarnation can we really know God in the riches of His fatherhood.

The Lord Keeps Pushing—Exodus 6:10-13

The Israelites did not respond to Moses' new promises of God for their deliverance. The increased bitter load of slavery was more real to them than God's fresh promises. God told Moses to return again to Pharaoh and issue another demand to let Israel go. Moses balked. Having heard the bitter words of the foremen (5:20,21), Moses had no heart to try again. Bad as the terrible slavery was now, Pharaoh might increase it if Moses persisted. So he replied that he had faltering lips (6:12). In other words, he was not eloquent. His ability to speak was no match for the surliness and fury of Pharaoh.

But God kept pushing! God knew the future. He knew what He would do. He knew that eventually Pharaoh would release Israel. So He told Moses to get with it! Granted, it is easy for us who know how the tale turns out to wonder at Moses. But if attempt number one turned out to be increased sufferings and not deliverance, why should Moses not have thought that this would also be the result of attempt number two? Would we have reasoned differently given the same circumstances? I think not. We share the same humanity with Moses. But always God is patient; His grace is greater than our immobility; and His love perseveres even when we fear. So, the Lord keeps pushing!

Connective Tissue Is Not Beautiful but It Is Necessary—Exodus 6:14-25

It may be asked why in the midst of a record of a great conflict a genealogical table is inserted. The reason is Israel's sense of history. Genealogical tables are history's connective tissue.

Animals are able to carry their heads more or less parallel to the ground and never tire because they have a special kind of tissue in their necks. This is called connective tissue. Man has connective tissue too but not so much as animals. Connective tissue is not beautiful like a face, but both man and beast would be in difficulty without it.

Israel's history begins with creation. As early as Genesis 4 and 5 we find genealogical lists. Israel had a profound sense of the continuity and unity of history. Each generation in some sense shared in all the past generations. This is the ultimate basis of typology and prophecy in Scripture. Israel's great religious festivals were to insure living generations that they participated in the great events of past generations.

These genealogical tables are found throughout the

Old Testament. Such tables are one of the ways this sense of participatory history is preserved. It is for this reason that Matthew and Luke give us genealogies of Christ. These genealogies are the connective tissue between the two Testaments.

Scripture is more than precious thoughts and pious sentiments. Scriptural revelation is anchored in history and genealogical tables, as graceless as they appear, and are firm pegs anchoring that revelation in history.

The Lord Must Push, Push, Push— Exodus 6:26—7:7

Most of the material of this section is restatement. It does underline the reticence of Moses to go before Pharaoh again. It reveals that the Lord who knows the outcome must push, push, push. And it does add to the tension building up to the plagues.

Again, we see the structure of revelation. Moses is to be God to Pharaoh (giving the divine Word) but Aaron actually speaks the Word. So the prophets are Aarons! They receive the divine Word from the Lord and speak it and write it to Israel. Through this process comes the divine Word in written form, the Old Testament.

The plagues are called "mighty acts of judgment" (7:4). It was wrong for the sons of Egypt's savior Joseph to be made slaves without cause. Originally it was the deed of Pharaoh but then the entire nation joined in oppressing Israel. Injustice is the summons for judgment. Modern man seeks to omit real judgment on the part of God and still preserve His love, but love in that case ceases to be holy love and disappears into sentiment and sentimentality.

This passage tells us that not only shall Israel know

that the Lord is God but so shall the Egyptians (7:5). This means that the Egyptians shall know that their great household of gods is a fiction. There is only one God of heaven and earth and, in the great contest coming, the Egyptians will learn that He is the Yahweh of the slaves. Again, this is in keeping with the nature of biblical religion. It is out of great historical events that the real nature of God becomes known.

In passing we are told that Moses is eighty years old and that Aaron is eighty-three. Hence we have the basis for dividing the life of Moses into forties: forty years in preparation, forty years in the wilderness, and forty years in service. D.L. Moody wittily said that Moses spent forty years in Pharaoh's court thinking he was somebody; forty years in the desert learning that he was nobody; and forty years showing what God can do with a somebody who found out he was a nobody.

4

He Is Able to Deliver Us

Exodus 7:8—11:10

The Show Gets on the Road—Exodus 7:8-13

Pharaoh, by the mercy of God, received one more chance to release Israel and avoid the plagues. If he had believed the importance of the sign he received he would have released Israel. Unfortunately he did not, but hardened his heart (7:13).

This passage initiates the action that will not end until Israel is safe on the far side of the Red Sea and the Egyptian army is drowned in the sea. It is therefore important to look at its typology all at once.

1. Pharaoh stands for all that oppresses man from without. It may be kings, his fellow men or Satan. In Scripture man is an oppressed being in need of divine deliverance.

2. Israel's slavery and bondage is the typology of all that oppresses man from within. In terms of Romans 7 and 8 it is the law of sin and death, or Paul's understanding of man as flesh, where *flesh* stands for all of man's depravity and weakness towards sin that manifests itself in specific acts of sin.

3. The plagues are symbols of God's wrath. It is God's wrath directed toward Pharaoh and the Egyptians as the oppressors of man—then towards all that is sinfully opposed to God.

4. The exodus experience is the typology of deliverance and redemption in all of Scripture. References to it appear in the Psalms, the prophets and in the New Testament.

5. The figure of Moses is the figure of the Deliverer and Redeemer. This fact is affirmed in Hebrews 3. The judges were Moses-like figures and so were the good kings in Israel and Judah. Christ is the fulfillment of this typology.

This is not allegorizing the text but picking up a typology of events that runs through all of Scripture. The Exodus is the archetype (the original, the masterpiece, the die from which all copies are struck) and model of divine deliverance.

Unless there is a deeper typology in Exodus, the story is trivial. There are hundreds of stories of struggle and survival in human history. What raises Exodus above them all is its deeper typology. The conflict is not only with the Pharaoh and the Egyptians but with their gods (see Exod. 12:12). It is deeper than that. It is with all gods, power, authorities, principalities and ideologies, visible or invisible, that oppose God and His truth and that enslave and oppress men. Hence one has to add the Christian typology, for here the struggle comes to its fullest realization and explication. To stop short of this is to reduce the Exodus struggle into the problem a number of Jewish tribes once had with a powerful old-world king.

The first encounter sets the pattern for the ten plagues. There is a time element here that is not always mentioned. It appears as though one event immediately follows another. Ignoring the time element introduces a burden on our credulity that disappears if we realize that the time element is obscured.

To begin with, the word "snake" is more generally translated sea monster and the Jewish commentators translated it "crocodile." Both snakes and crocodiles have been paralyzed by magicians in recent times. Snakes may be paralyzed by bending the head back; when tossed on the ground they lose their stick-like rigidity and slither off.

The old world was a world of magicians and superstition. We know that the art of magic was skillfully developed in ancient Egypt. We can see the direct import of the story. The "magicians" of the slave people whose God is Yahweh can outsmart and overpower the magicians of the oppressive Pharaoh and his pantheon of gods.

Nine Strokes at Pharaoh, the Egyptians and Their Gods—Exodus 7:14—10:29

Pharaoh had resisted all efforts of Moses to get the captive peoples released. The issue now had to be forced. It would take ten plagues before Pharaoh would give the command to let Israel go.

Plagues are common occurrences in Egypt, only now they were to occur in a sudden and heightened form. They are called "signs and wonders" (7:3) because in this instance they were wrought by the agency of God. They are called judgments of God (see Exod. 12:12) because they were the manifestation of the wrath of God against the Egyptians for the illegal forcing of Israel into slavery. The last plague, announced in Exodus 11:1, is called a *stroke* in Hebrew because it involved the death of the most precious member of the Egyptian family, the firstborn.

These terrible plagues were not soon forgotten but were remembered by Israel and surrounding peoples (see Deut. 4:34; 7:19; Josh. 24:5; 1 Sam. 4:8; Pss. 78:43-51; 135:9; Jer. 32:21). They were a terrifying experience for all who passed through them—no wonder that they left a lasting impression on that ancient world.

Commentators generally agree that the plagues basically represent a contest between Moses as the representative of Yahweh and Pharaoh as the representative of the gods of Egypt. Efforts have been made to find the religious dimension for each plague although there is no agreement on this:

1. The Nile was considered a god by the Egyptians and to turn it into blood or a reddish mess of dirt and algae was an insult to the river as a god.
2. There was a frog god named *Heka* or *Heket.*
3. According to some, gnats polluted the temple, so the plague of gnats was an insult to the temple of gods it housed. Another interpretation is that *Seth* was the god of earth and that this plague would insult him by polluting the earth.
4. If the fly is actually the sacred beetle, then this plague is an insult to the god *Khepra.*
5. Cattle, especially horses, were sacred to the Egyptians and highly venerated and so worshiped.
6. Soot was used by the priests to bless the people. This plague would turn a blessing into a curse. Others associate this plague with *Neit,* the great mother of heaven.
7. *Isis* and *Serapis* were the gods of fire and water, yet they could not protect Egypt from hail.
8. These gods were also to protect Egypt from locusts and they could not.

9. The darkness was aimed at *Ra,* the sun God, and for *Set,* the evil principle who could cause darkness.

10. The Pharaoh was considered divine so the tenth plague was against the divine heir to the throne.

The text simply lumps all the Egyptian gods together and says that God's judgment is against them (see 12:12). The preceding remarks are interesting speculation but cannot be proved. They suggest, however, how the Egyptians might have understood the plagues as insults to their entire religious system. The conclusion is obvious: Yahweh, the God of the slaves, is superior to the pantheon of Egyptian gods.

All commentators agree that these plagues were heightened occurrences of the kinds of events that from time to time plagued Egypt. The Nile at times is reddish and hard to drink from because of its burden of soil and algae. Frogs, lice, animal diseases and so on can all be substantiated as typical of the plagues Egypt suffered from naturally. But these plagues were different from ordinary phenomena of a similar nature in that: (a) they were controlled as to their occurrence and disappearance by Moses and the Word of God; (b) their intensity was greatly increased; (c) Israel was providentially spared from them.

The real question is: What was the nature of the plagues that made them fit so providentially into the release of Israel? Here opinions differ sharply.

1. Some say that they are pure fabrications of later writers in Israel. If one takes the biblical revelation seriously, as we do, this is no solution. This is the modern "Enlightenment" mentality that allows for no divine participation in the history of Israel and it destroys the authority of Scripture.

2. One may say that the plagues are pure miracles of

God. This is possible but most commentators do not favor this view. Each of the plagues did occur at other times in Egypt's history so there is a strong natural element to each plague. Again this is in keeping with the nature of cultural accommodation in revelation. God does not strike the Egyptians with plagues known only to Eskimos or Hottentots.

3. The plagues were a combination of natural phenomena known to both the Egyptians and Israelites alike (due to their long sojourn in Egypt) heightened by the addition of supernatural factors. This is our position.[1]

4. The plagues were ordinary phenomena. In the history of Israel they were later schematized and made highly dramatic. The supernatural element is purely in their coincidental nature. They were, then, "miracles of coincidence." This position is supposed to lessen the pull on our credulity and at the same time maintain God's sovereign action, His work of grace and the reality of divine relation in our world.

There is no question that the account is highly dramatized. Again, the time element is not always specifically stated and condensation gives the appearance of sudden, miraculous occurrence. The author wants the account to be dramatic. He wants to show the real, immediate conflict of Yahweh and Pharaoh. To show the sharp edge of this conflict, secondary items must be dropped out. No historian is faulted for exercising the principle of selectivity if he informs us what he is doing and why. The intent here is to show the great contest going on and the purpose is to show Yahweh as greater than all the gods of Egypt. Dramatizing and schematizing may heighten the miraculous element and we must take account of this.

Another aspect of the account of these nine plagues is

the sad picture of Pharaoh. He is like a beginner taking on an Olympic champion. His vacillations under pressure are pathetic. Those who resist God are more to be pitied for their folly than scolded for their unbelief.

The plagues also reveal how great the Lord God of Israel is: "It will be as you say, so that you may know there is no one like the LORD our God" (8:10).

Redemption over evil powers and Satan is a side issue in the New Testament but it is there. It is manifest first in our Lord's public ministry in His power to cast out the stooges of Satan. And then in His death we are told that "Having disarmed the powers and authorities, he made a public spectacle of them, triumphing over them by the cross" (Col. 2:15).

As predicted, in reaction to the plagues Pharaoh hardened his heart (7:13). As mean as Pharaoh was toward the Israelites we pity this man. Like Paul before his conversion he kicked mightily against the ox-goads of God. This led to disaster for him and for the Egyptians. He seemed opaque to the competition he had taken head on. We now see what hardness of heart means. For Pharaoh it meant the failure to see in many signs the truth that Yahweh was a far more powerful God than all the gods of the Egyptians.

The Final Plague—the Stroke that Shakes Pharaoh Loose—Exodus 11:1-10

A special word is used in Hebrew for the last plague: *a stroke.* That means a plague more disastrous than any of the former nine.

One critical theory is that a childhood disease spread among the children in Egypt and that many died. Later in the history of Israel, according to this theory, the facts were sharpened into the story before us. The disease was limited to the firstborn of the Egyptians; and it struck suddenly one night.

Such an effort to reduce the catastrophic nature of this plague to something natural and more acceptable causes problems. For the biblical story hangs together. If the story is watered down by substituting an epidemic for a plague, the cause-and-effect relationship is destroyed. Certainly the Pharaoh depicted in Exodus would not have released Israel because of an ordinary epidemic among children.

Further, the very essence of the story is the place of the firstborn son in that culture; it is known as the right of primogeniture. Primogeniture means that the chief heir to a man, his property, his name and his rights was his firstborn son. In such a culture the oldest son was the most important of all children. Therefore to strike down the firstborn would be a singular tragedy. An epidemic among all children could not match it as a plague or a stroke or a national catastrophe.

Another feature of this plague is that it was accomplished by the direct action of God Himself. It was therefore a unique judgment of God, different from the previous plagues and marked an increase in the severity of the plagues. In this plague human beings died and this could be the responsibility only of God, the Judge of all flesh.

It was also the final triumph over the gods of Egypt: "I will bring judgment on all the gods of Egypt. I am the LORD" (12:12). This is not always obvious in the record and is not stated explicitly until 12:12. But it is there all the time. As indicated in the discussion of the plagues each plague can be interpreted as an insult to one or more of the gods of Egypt. The plagues represent the first great encounter of the monotheistic, non-idolatrous faith of Israel with an old-world empire, its pantheon of gods and its idolatry. Clearly it was a momentous thing for all of history that a monotheistic faith won the contest with the polytheism of a great, ancient kingdom.

The last plague struck at midnight. The only reason offered for midnight is that according to Egyptian mythology, it was the time the gods fought. If this was the backdrop then it would be a natural that Yahweh and the gods of Egypt would struggle for mastery at the midnight hour. The winner was obviously Yahweh.

The last plague was also a great judgment (12:12). This judgment was signed by the statement: "I am the LORD." This is a common Old Testament saying. It means that the highest court has spoken. No higher appeal can be made; no greater authority can be cited in support. It is also an affirmation of absolute wisdom, equity and righteousness. It is beyond contention. Those who contest the ethical propriety of the plagues must first explain the inadequacy of "I am the LORD."

The death of the firstborn was a major catastrophe. Especially it was a disaster for Pharaoh and the religion of Egypt. The heir to the throne was called *erpa suten sa*—"the hereditary crown prince." Upon ascending the throne he would become a divine ruler. To strike him dead meant not only the great personal loss of the first son but also the death of the divine heir apparent, and further, a blow at the religion of the Egyptians. It was such a catastrophic blow that it made Pharaoh's hard heart give in. If he further resisted might not his own life be the next plague?

The plague was universal from Pharaoh's house to that of the slave girl who worked in the mill (an Egyptian phrase for "the poorest of the poor") to the cattle in the field. The first reason for this universality is that all of Egypt had joined in the enslavement of Israel, so all of Egypt must suffer the judgment. The second reason is to reinforce the truth that God is no respecter of persons. The rich are not exempt for their high status in society and the poor are not exempt because of their hard lot. The third reason is that in the great typology of the book of Exodus it speaks of the universality of the judgment of God. As Paul says *the whole world* comes before the judgment of God (see Rom. 3:19) and as the book of Revelation affirms, the dead "great and small" (20:12) shall stand before God in judgment.

Another bit of local color is added to the Exodus account when it says that "not a dog will bark" (11:7) against the Israelites. They are the redeemed and elect. Judgment does not come their way. The reason is given: "The LORD makes a distinction between Egypt and Israel" (v. 7).

That is it! The Lord makes the difference. Israel is not in any way superior to Egypt. The book of Deuteronomy repeatedly says that Israel was chosen by God's grace and love, not on the basis of any superiority Israel possessed over other nations. Israel did not make herself different. Only God can make a distinction among sinners of equal depravity and guilt.

How true this is in the light of the New Testament. Christians are Christians because of God's grace and Christ's redemption. Christians are not more intelligent than non-Christians, nor more pure, nor more sensitive religiously, nor higher in any other category of excellence that man may suggest. God makes the difference in Jesus Christ.

No dog will bark against the Christian! Such an affirmation occurs twice in Romans 8. In the first verse it is said that there is no condemnation to them that are in Christ Jesus. Then in verses 33,34 we are told that nobody can successfully bring a charge against the redeemed. Again, no dog will bark not because Christians can make themselves different from non-Christians, but because God makes the difference for Christians in Christ.

The mood of contemporary theology is universalistic. We are told that there is no distinction between Israel and Egypt. Both are in the ark by virtue of God's universal love. If this is the case, evangelism and missions should consist of *informing* non-Christians that they are already in the ark of safety and merely should adopt the Christian way of faith and life.

No doubt the love of God is universal for John 3:16 includes the whole world in it. Certainly God's intentions are universalistic, for He is unwilling that any should perish but desires that all should come to a knowledge of the truth (see 2 Pet. 3:9 and 1 Tim. 2:4). Further the church is invited to reconcile the world in Christ (see 2 Cor. 5:19). But as a matter of fact, all do not believe in the name of Christ and receive eternal love. All do not repent and come to a knowledge of the truth. All do not accept the message of reconciliation and come into peace with God. The Lord still makes a difference among men and as hard as limited salvation seems it does secure the enormous distinction salvation makes among the children of men.

Notes

1. The following summarizes some of our knowledge of the plagues insofar as they are natural phenomena in Egypt.

a. *Nile.* At the flooding season the Nile carries much red earth and small bacteria giving it a red ochre color and a foul smell (flagellates, algae, etc.). This flooding is from around July and August to around October and November.

b. *Frogs.* The increase of frogs after the overflow of the Nile is well-documented. They can eat the decaying fish and also catch any disease or bacteria the fish may have.

c. *Dust to gnats or mosquitoes.* The immense increase of mosquitoes with overflow of the Nile leaving endless pools of water and the dead carcasses of frogs would naturally follow. Some have thought that the dust-turned-to-mosquitoes would be an insult to the god of the earth, *Seb,* or to the sacred black earth of Egypt called *Chemi.*

d. *Flies.* Again flies would be a natural consequence of the flooding of the Nile and the dead frogs.

e. *Cattle plague or murrain.* Terrible blights of cattle disease were experienced in modern times in Egypt in 1842, 1863 and 1866. Again the conditions of the land after the retreat of the stinking Nile from the first plague would foster a disease among the cattle. The Israelites apparently kept their cattle in sheds and so avoided the disease.

f. *Boils.* These are caused most likely by a skin anthrax. They could also be traced to the Nile and the dead frogs. Some have thought that there was an insult here to the gods *Sutech* or *Typhon.*

g. *Hail.* As cloudless as Egypt appears most of the time it can experience thunderstorms with hail. To people who live in almost perpetual sunshine such a storm would be exceedingly fearful. Storms occur in the winter and as late as March.

h. *Locusts.* We know from the Old Testament how terrible locusts are. They literally strip a countryside to stumps, stones and dirt. They were considered the most terrible of insect plagues in that ancient world.

i. *Darkness.* In a dust storm known as the *Khamsa* fine particles are drifted by the wind; it is said that it is denser than fog and that it can be felt. Although such storms may drift around for a month their intensity is in three-day spells (Exod. 10:23).

j. *Death of the firstborn.* Some commentators think that ordinary children's diseases were involved here. Some unusual scourge with many deaths may have constituted the historical background that gave rise to the story of the death of the firstborn. This theory is considered in the exposition of Exodus 11 that follows.

5

We're Redeemed by the Blood

Exodus 12:1-28

How Israel Escapes the Tenth Plague—Exodus 12:1-13

The tenth plague so shook Pharaoh and the Egyptians that they released Israel. Accordingly much more space is given to it than to the preceding plagues. Further, the deeper typology comes into play with the tenth plague in that Israel had to do something too—sacrifice a lamb. Certain national feasts were inaugurated with the Passover and they must be narrated in some detail.

The fact that a typology is present in the tenth plague is stated in 1 Corinthians 5:7: "Get rid of the old yeast that you may be a new batch without yeast—as you really are. For Christ, our Passover lamb, has been sacrificed [for us]."

The tenth plague was the death either of the firstborn or of a lamb. It was the Lord who moved through the land passing over the places where there was the sign of the blood but slaying the firstborn where it was absent (Exod. 12:23). It was also a judgment on the gods of Egypt (12:12) for it showed that they could not protect their worshipers, the Egyptians. In this most serious of conflicts, between life or death, Yahweh again showed that He is the living God, and the gods of the Egyptians but dead pieces of stone or wood or precious metal.

The typological element centers on the threat of judgment and the alleviation of that judgment through the death of a lamb. It is for this reason that Paul speaks of Christ's death as the true fulfillment of the Passover lamb. He is the Lamb of God who takes away our sin and so removes the basis for our judgment (see John 1:29). When commentators attempt to explain the passage in terms of possible old-world mythology or later Jewish customs they trivialize the entire exodus experience. Instead of representing the triumph of Yahweh over the forces of Egypt and their gods as the great typology of redemption and deliverance for Israel and the church, the account becomes a confused story of the obscure escape of some Jewish slaves from Egypt whose religion was not yet free from animism.

Each man who was the head of a household (so functioning as a priest) was to take a lamb, slay it, eat some of it roasted, burn the rest and put blood around the wood supports of his door (Exod. 12:7). This was an act of faith (see Heb. 11:28). Here again we see the deepening typology. This tenth plague had no automatic exemption for the Hebrews. It was a great day of judgment on all—it was the blood of the sacrifice that saved Israel. But as Hebrews 11:28 suggests, they kept the Passover in faith. Externally the blood of the Passover was the difference the Lord made; internally it was faith. How true this is to the New Testament pattern.

Furthermore it was *the Lord's* Passover (Exod. 12:11). This means that whatever Israel may have practiced by way of putting blood on tents or houses or temples was now behind. The ritual had a new significance. It had the significance the Lord gave it. Further, it wasn't some trick or stunt or ritual made up by the Israelites. It was something specified and interpreted by the Lord. This should be an answer to those who still see it as some sort of primitive animism where blood was put on tent flaps to keep out of the tent at night evil spirits who might be intent on killing the inhabitants.

To jump to the New Testament, the cross was no invention of the disciples nor the early church to rescue the tragic death of Christ from oblivion. The cross was God's provision, not man's manipulation. This is the frequent meaning of "hour" in the Gospel of John. Our Lord kept an appointment at the cross, His hour, and it was a divine appointment just as the lamb of the exodus was by divine prescription.

This exodus is a rescue, a redemption and a salvation. Here is the basis for the writers of the entire Old Testament and of the New Testament to consider the Exodus as the great typology of divine salvation.

The blood on the door was a sign (12:13). A sign of what? Certainly a sign that the lamb had been slain. It was also a sign that the household within had acted on faith. It was further a sign for the Destroyer (12:23) to pass by. So redemption in Christ is the sign of the believer. The sign of the fish is a very old Christian symbol; but the sign of the cross is deeper for that is the sign of Christ our Passover, slain for us.

The Memorial of the Exodus for All Generations—Exodus 12:14-20

From a loose association of twelve tribes, Israel was to be formed into one nation by the Exodus. All subsequent generations of Israelites would be heirs of this great event. In a realistic way the Old Testament saw all of Israel sharing in these great events. This sharing was made real by the concept of re-presentation. By re-presenting the original event through ritual and ceremony, subsequent generations participated in the original event. The parallels here with Christian baptism and Christian communion are very close.

At this point the festival of unleavened bread, which lasted seven days, is introduced. It was to be binding on all subsequent generations of Israelites for it was a memorial day (12:14) and an ordinance (12:24). In this festival the manner in which the Israelites prepared for and awaited their deliverance *from* Pharaoh *into* life as God's free people was reenacted. In this reenactment there is re-presentation of this phase of the exodus experience.

The exodus experience was also the start of the new year for Israel (12:2). In a sense Israel had two calendars just as people in our culture do. People in business may have a fiscal year differing from the calendar year, just as people in education have an academic year and people in sports have the seasonal year. So Israel had an agricultural year with its new year in the springtime and their new year of redemption in the month of Nisan.

That the Exodus should start a new year tells us something about how God begins human life again. God's New Year begins with redemption. God's New Year is different from our calendar year and different from our birthday when we mark our own personal year. God's New Year begins with the new birth (see John 3:3,5). New life in Christ is God's New Year.

Yeast was to be excluded. The reason for this is not stated in the text. The implication is that in a time of haste there was no time to let bread rise. Unleavened bread is the bread of the pilgrim who is ready to continue his march at any time. To leaven one's bread was to risk not being ready when the word to march came, hence a sign of unbelief. There is Old Testament, rabbinic, classical literature and New Testament support for yeast meaning something that corrupts. Paul gives it such a connotation in referring to the Passover (see 1 Cor. 5:7). Such understandings come later in Hebrew tradition.

An understanding of the festivals of Israel can enlarge our understanding of the Christian sacraments. They are not so much "means of grace" as in sacramentarian theology, nor ordinances or institutions of a purely symbolic function. Rather, they are re-presentations of the great act of our redemption with the express purpose of showing that we and our children are somehow *there* participating not only in their meaning but also in the blessings they proffer. "Let us keep the festival" (1 Cor. 5:8).

Israel Accepts the Terms of the Passover And So Acts—Exodus 12:21-28

What God related to Moses (12:1-20) was now told to the elders of Israel (12:21) who in turn related it to the heads of all the families. The Israelites were assured that if the blood of the lamb was on the doorposts they would be protected from "the destroyer" when the tenth plague struck (12:23).

This plague was not like the other nine. It was the stroke that was at the same time judgment to Egypt and salvation to Israel. Accordingly it was an event that lay at the foundation of Israel. If preparation for the event became a national perpetual holiday so did the great event itself. It was, then, made "a lasting ordinance for you and your descendants" (12:24).

We have noted that as the event of divine redemption, the Passover and the Exodus became the fundamental type of divine redemption in all of Scripture. The return from the exile has been called a second exodus, and as we have seen, the death of Christ is another exodus. As the primary event of deliverance and redemption it means that all of Israel participates in it. Therefore, like the feast of unleavened bread it is a re-presentation, a reenactment in order that other generations may accept it by an act of faith and so participate in its meaning and blessings.

It is a festival of reenactment, participation and instruction. The children of subsequent generations will ask about it; then they will be told its meaning. How much more effective this kind of instruction is than so much of our teaching in our churches done in the artificial setting of a Sunday School class.

The Israelites bowed their heads in grateful worship and then followed the instructions of Moses. This was an act of faith as Hebrews 11:28 suggests. As great as the Passover promises were, and as mighty as the work of the Lord was that night, they only became truth, reality and experience as they were responded to in faith. This is in keeping with the total biblical revelation that only by faith can we please God (see Heb. 11:6) and make His promises effective for ourselves.

This is also true of that great and final exodus, the cross. No matter how much love was revealed in the cross and no matter how great salvation was brought there, none of it comes through to man apart from faith. Faith is the living bond between Creator and creature, Lord and servant, Father and son and without it there is no religion as the holy Scripture understands religion.

6

I'm Free Because He's Faithful

Exodus 12:29—15:21

It Happens—the Blow of the Tenth Plague Falls—Exodus 12:29-39

For at least eighty years (the age of Moses at this time) all the male babies in Israel that the Egyptians could apprehend had been killed. Now the tenth plague came as a judgment on that special act of cruelty as well as the supreme judgment on the gods of Egypt whose human representative was Pharaoh.

The Destroyer left the mark of death from the firstborn in the Big House of Pharaoh to the firstborn of the lowest in the land—here stated as the captive in prison. With the discovery of the dead children a great cry went up in Egypt as household after household awakened to find its dead. Loud cries of great armies have been heard for some miles and this must have been a cry like that.

How tragic that men must discover the bitter way that God is not only a God of grace, love, redemption and gentle providence but also a God of holiness, justice, wrath and judgment. If He were not *holy* love, His love would degenerate into senseless affection. If men could not experience wrath as well as love, then life would become bland and trivial. It would become a pastime and not the essence of seriousness. Redemption would not really be redemption but more like decorations added to an already frosted cake.

At last Aaron and Moses heard the words for which they had patiently waited through nine plagues in which Pharaoh had repeatedly hardened his heart: "Go, worship the LORD" (12:31). Now the yoke was loosened, the chains broken, the manacles struck free! And what a concluding word: "and also bless me" (v. 32).

Why this statement: "and also bless me"? Because Pharaoh had had his fill of plagues! If God could curse this way, how great must be His blessings? There is also an implication: "Let your God heal my land after all the terrible plagues." What a transformation has taken place from the first surly "Who is Yahweh?" to "also bless me." Look at this picture slowly. A proud, powerful monarch of one of the great old-world kingdoms asks the blessing of the God of his slaves. It was not really Moses triumphing over Pharaoh, but the Lord. And it was a triumph not only over Pharaoh but over the gods of Egypt.

The Egyptians apparently thought that the plague was just beginning and that before it was through "we will all die!" (v. 33). They were more than anxious for the Israelites to leave and willingly gave them their valuable jewelry and clothing. Quite a transformation had taken place here too! The Egyptian populace had carried out the cruel edicts of Pharaoh. They had oppressed, beaten and even murdered the Israelites. Now they fear for their lives because of the lowly slaves. Here again the transformation must be attributed to Yahweh, and Yahweh alone.

The Israelites moved to Rameses and Succoth which

have been tentatively identified in the land of Goshen. They were now on their way to the Promised Land! The covenantal promises made to Abraham were now beginning to come true.

The travelers included "many other people" (v. 38). We do not know for sure who they were. Some guess old Semites, others think Hebrews in the wider sense of a large number of migrants to Egypt and others believe captives in Egypt from other peoples who took advantage of the edict to let all slaves go.

Even More Ways of Remembering the Great Night of the Exodus—Exodus 12:40—13:16

So great was the deliverance of Israel, an enslaved nation, from a great world power that it was to be thoroughly remembered in Israel. It marked, as we have emphasized, the founding of Israel as a nation—an event in which all other generations of Israel should partake. It is also the great typology of redemption in Christ according to the New Testament. Therefore God established many ways to ensure its remembrance in Israel. Exodus 12:40—13:16 is rich in those ways.

1. Because the Passover was a night of watching by the Lord, there is to be a night of watching kept *to* the Lord by all the people of Israel through their generations (12:42). This is another way of referring to the keeping of the Passover.

2. Further, this Passover belongs only to covenant-keepers, i.e., Israelites who have been circumcised and sojourners who have been converted to the faith of Israel and circumcised. The Passover would be meaningless to a person outside the Abrahamic covenant.

3. Deeply typical and symbolic, although it could not

be known to Israel at that time, was that not a bone of the Passover lamb was to be broken. John finds this fulfilled in the early death of our Lord so that His legs were not splintered with hammers to hasten death (see John 19:36).

4. Most space is given to the claim that all the firstborn of men and animals belong to God. It was the firstborn who were slain in the tenth plague among the Egyptians but spared among the Israelites. In order to impress this great tenth plague on all the generations of Israel, God instituted the requirement that the Israelites redeem all firstborn of men and animals with a price. Such a practice vigorously followed would make the exodus event truly unforgettable in the history of Israel. It was also to be a point of departure for again instructing their children in the great exodus experience.

5. Finally, whether meant literally or metaphorically, there were to be signs of the event in the hands and forehead of the Israelites. Jewish scholars take this to be the ultimate origin and justification for binding verses from the law (Torah) on their arms and foreheads. Many Protestant commentators take the expressions of Exodus 13:9 and 16 metaphorically.

Either way the real point is made in verse 9: "that the law of the LORD is to be on your lips." That means that the story of divine, miraculous redemption from Egypt should be told *readily* again and again and again.

From this the Christian church may learn several things: first, the value of yearly Christian festivals to tell the story of our Lord—His birth, life, death and resurrection—again and again; second, the importance of the sacraments as the "visible words of God" telling in another way the great message of redemption through Christ; and third, the need to have the Word of God, the message of the gospel, the sound of reconciliation always ready in our mouths to convey to our children and our neighbors.

The Israelites Begin the March to Palestine—Exodus 13:17-22

The closest route from Goshen to Palestine was a sandy, desert route taking about two weeks to transit. But it was a heavily fortified route. To avoid plunging Israel into a series of wars more devastating than Egyptian slavery, God turned them southward for a much longer but safer route (Exod. 13:17,18).

Further, the Israelites were not a disorganized mob but went out of Egypt "armed for battle." The expression includes not only the concept of weapons but the idea of military organization. It reflects Moses' experience in the court of Pharaoh where he could have learned some military arts, because as the son of Pharaoh's daughter he had been "educated in all the wisdom of the Egyptians" (Acts 7:22).

Their route was towards the Red Sea[1] which was already setting a trap for the Egyptian army.

By Joseph's request they took his bones with them (Exod. 13:19). Here we see what was understood by Joseph and the Hebrews but is not explicitly stated in the text. Joseph, Moses and the Hebrews believed the Abrahamic promises. They would occupy the land of the Philistines and the Canaanites. Was there also a meaning deeper than that? Does Joseph's request suggest some thoughts of the afterlife for which his bones would be important? In Hebrews 11:22 we are told that Joseph anticipated the Exodus and made mention of the care of his bones *by faith!* He certainly envisioned something more important than the reburial of his bones. Somehow he would participate in the profounder meaning of the Abrahamic promises as Paul discusses them in Galatians.

Next we are told that the Lord went before the hosts of Israel guiding them by a pillar of cloud by day and by a pillar of fire by night (Exod. 13:21,22). Evidently the Israelites had forced marches to put as much distance as possible between them and Pharaoh. It was customary for armies in that ancient world to be guided by smoke and fire signals; they did not have radios or other methods of rapid communication. Smoking and burning braziers were lifted up on tall poles and carried before armies.[2]

It was necessary for Israel to be guided safely away from Pharaoh and away from warring peoples and fortresses. God providentially provided His own manifestation to guide them. This means that we can never separate providence from salvation. How odd it would be of God to save His people in a *special* way and then turn them loose to the churnings of the world. Not so. Whom God redeems He cares for. Those who come under the wing of His salvation, come under the care of His special providence. This is true not only of Israel in the Old Testament but of Christians in the New Testament.

The Final Spasm of Pharaoh and the Great Triumph of Yahweh—Exodus 14:1-31

The silent force in the shadow of all of Israel's time of slavery had been the Egyptian army. It was destroyed in the Red Sea as the final humiliation of Egypt and the great salvation of Israel (v. 13). Redemption by the sacrifice of a lamb and the blood on the door supports was followed by redemption by power at the Red Sea.

With the transit through the Red Sea and the destruction of Pharaoh's army Israel was now a free, united nation. She was on her way to her inheritance in Palestine. The great deliverance was now a fact. All the promises made by the Lord about it were fulfilled. Next on the agenda would be the march into the land of covenantal promise.

As soon as the initial grief over the death of the firstborn subsided, Pharaoh realized his loss of his slaves—a standard possession and source of labor and power for old-world kings. So again with a hardened heart (v. 4) he set out in pursuit of Israel with his army and his elite guard of six hundred chariots and other chariots. These chariots usually carried three men—one to drive the horses and the other two to fight.

In this last encounter between Egypt and Israel God would get the glory (v. 4). "Glory" means something external; something that can be viewed by the eye; something manifest and not hidden; something that brings fame, honor and good report. So the honor that Yahweh got was the destruction of the Egyptian army visible to all of Israel (v. 30).

When the Israelites saw Pharaoh's army approaching they were terrified and cried out to the Lord (v. 10). Then they complained to Moses that they would sooner have lived out their lives in Egypt and been buried there than be ruthlessly slain by soldiers in the wilderness. This murmuring of the Israelites occurs throughout the book of Exodus so we must deal with it here.

Why did the Israelites who saw the great power and remarkable providences of God murmur against their God?

1. Not all the company were Israelites. As noted, a

mixed multitude came out of Egypt with Israel (12:38). These people could have been the source of the murmuring. Further, not all the Israelites were equally men of faith. Paul says that not all Israelites nationally are Israelites spiritually (see Rom. 9:6). The murmuring could be from the purely nationalistic Israelites.

2. At that time Israel had no Scripture as we understand Scripture. They had no sense of the whole history of redemption and revelation. Hence the ways of God were very obscure and difficult to them. Such people could easily murmur out of their restricted understanding.

3. As slave people they were not as a whole educated or learned people. They were people who lived close to the edge of existence. Food, water, weather, disease and epidemics were always pressing realities. They would feel the threat of the loss of food and water or the impending disaster of disease and so on very keenly. Their fear could easily make them a murmuring people.

This is not to say that by comparison the history of the church is glorious. The days of proving Christianity by the glories of church history are near an end. Historians know too many sordid pages of church history. Christians also are capable of murmuring as well as of unbelievable mistakes of judgment, errors in ethical perception, "holy wars" and acts of barbarism. Torturing criminals had Christian sanction for many centuries.

The Christian does note that justification is not glorification nor is regeneration perfection. Christians are still in unregenerate flesh and capable of all its evil deeds. Further, the Christian affirms that his righteousness is of Christ and not his own.

Moses' answer to the murmuring Israelites was for them to stand firm and be still and see the salvation of the

Lord (Exod. 14:13,14). These are remarkable verses. Moses claimed as great a deliverance from the might of the Egyptian army as from the Destroyer by midnight. The Egyptians Israel saw that day would never be seen again—alive!

The transit through the Red Sea is partially dependent on which body of water was the Red Sea. Phenomena similar to that described in this fourteenth chapter have been observed in the lakes between the present Red Sea and the Mediterranean. There is also the possibility that the northern end of the Red Sea was many miles further inland so that the place of transit is now under sand. And there is the question whether the wall of water (14:22) is to be taken literally or figuratively as it may be in 15:8.

The transit of the sea was similar to the plagues. There was a natural element ("and all at that night the LORD drove the sea back with a strong east wind," 14:21) and there was a supernatural element (in the obedience of the sea to the command of Moses both to open and to return to its normal flow and the manner in which the waters piled up).

Any naturalistic explanation does not do justice to the text. It cannot all be explained by a "miracle of coincidence" nor by "the eyes of faith." As we have propounded before, such a view may seem to make peace for some commentators with the uniformity of nature and the scientific mentality.

But it asks for serious trouble from another direction. Historians and others guided by hard criteria of factuality will say that to call the event a miracle of coincidence or some natural phenomenon transformed by the eyes of faith into a great act of God is to really assert that nothing unusual or supernatural happened.

That the Hebrews and the Egyptians thought directly of the action of God and not in terms of secondary causes is seen in verses 24,25. It is said that the Lord clogged the wheels of the chariots so that the Egyptians could not catch the Israelites. It was the secondary cause, the mud and sand, that did this.

Verses 30 and 31 are a marvelous conclusion to the episode. The Egyptians who so bitterly persecuted the Israelites were found dead on the shore the next morning. When the murmuring people saw that, they "feared the LORD and put their trust in him and in Moses his servant" (v. 31). The deliverance from Egypt and the Egyptians was now complete.

There is a similar mood to be found in the Gospel account of the death and resurrection of our Lord. There is the persecution of Jews and Gentiles intent on His death. There is the despairing event of the Crucifixion. There are the bewildering hours from Friday night to Sunday morning. Then there is the report of the Resurrection which at first the disciples considered as "nonsense" (Luke 24:11). Finally, the risen Lord appears and all is joy and peace.

Redemption is a real thing. There are ripples in this world of ours made by the presence and activity of the living God. Many theologians and philosophers object to these supernatural ripples on the surface of our history. But if they were not there would there really be such a thing as Christianity? Is not faith then pure subjective conviction with no credible object? If there are no ripples, God makes no difference whether He is denied or believed. For our house we confess the greatest ripple of all: "But Christ has indeed been raised from the dead" (1 Cor. 15:20).

From the Groanings of Egypt to the Song of Redemption—Exodus 15:1-21

On reaching the safe side of the Red Sea and seeing the bodies of the drowned Egyptian soldiers on the beach, Israel sang, danced and played tambourines (v. 20). The significance of the tambourine is that it was a percussion instrument used especially in times of great joy.

When does man turn to poetry, music and dance? He does so in times of great emotional excitement or stirrings. Ordinary prose fails to carry the burden of feeling. The ordinary voice of speech seems flat and unequal to the occasion. The joy that fills the heart demands that the whole body respond in dance.

The feelings and emotions of the Israelites were at a maximum! They had known the bitterness of slavery with its beatings, its drudgery and its murders. Now they were free from all that for the army of the Pharaoh had been humiliated and drowned! How else could they express such excitement and joy than by moving from prose to poetry, from speaking to singing and from walking to dancing? This is what the wonderful experience of salvation does to people!

So it is in the New Testament. When a Christian is filled with the Spirit, this means the excitation of emotion and feeling, but not for the sake of the feeling and the emotion. These are the products of something else, namely, the filling of the Spirit. This joy expresses itself in psalms, hymns and spiritual songs. "Sing and make music in your heart to the Lord" (Eph. 5:19), Paul encourages.

In the book that is filled with far more gruesome events than the book of Exodus, the book of Revelation, singing is mentioned three times as a response to God's great salvation (see Rev. 5:9; 14:3; 15:3). It is the joy of

Christ, in ordinary or extraordinary times, that has created Christian hymnology. It is a unique phenomenon among the religions of the world. Christianity is the "singingest" of all religions. The Pietists of Germany alone produced in excess of 200,000 hymns. There is a reason! It is redemption, salvation and deliverance that sets the heart singing. All the Psalms are words to songs. The roots of the phenomenon are in the Old Testament; the maturity is in the New Testament.

The song of Exodus 15 falls into two parts, verses 1-12 and 13-18. The first part centers on the redemption from Egypt; the second on the entrance into Palestine. Some scholars think that the second part is of later composition because it anticipates later events and Israel's establishment in the land. However, in the concept of enlargement of earlier themes by a later community as they saw the earlier events in greater depth, this poses no problem. The pattern set all the way through Exodus is that the total exodus experience is always *from* Egypt and *into* Palestine. This is the theme echoed in the New Testament, too, as we have indicated. Redemption is always *from* our sin, guilt and depravity *into* new life in Christ and in the Holy Spirit.

The song is filled with poetic descriptions, figures of speech and metaphors—all characteristic of the elevated nature of poetry. One of the excellent verses is 15:11.

"Who among the gods [of Egypt] is like you, O LORD?

Who is like you—majestic in holiness, awesome in glory, working wonders?"

The basis of this redemption was divine *chesed*—"unfailing love" (v. 13). *Chesed*[3] is a very Hebrew word. It has no ready equivalent in Greek or English. It combines ideas of loyalty, steadfastness, mercy and love. It is a strong covenantal word. God maintains his covenant with man by His *chesed.* It somewhat parallels the Greek, *agape*—divine, forgiving, accepting, redemptive love.

The song ends with the words, "The LORD will reign for ever and ever" (v. 18). The whole Exodus experience is a commentary on what the reign of God is. He reigns through the way in which He executes judgment and salvation! The beginnings of the concept of the Kingdom of God are in the Old Testament. It is the concept of the Kingdom that unites the themes of salvation, church and eschatology in the New Testament. We must be careful that we do not think of the reign of God totally in terms of the future, either of the millennium or of heaven. The Kingdom of God has come, is coming and will come!

Notes

1. Much research has gone into the attempt to locate the Red Sea. The term Reed Sea (*eruthan thalassan*) occurs first in the Greek translation of the Old Testament (the Septuagint). Red Sea occurs in the New Testament in Acts 7:36 and Hebrews 11:29. The expression is a general one used for a variety of waters, so nothing can be determined by the expression itself.

It has been suggested that "red" derives from red rushes around a body of water. If it means papyrus reeds then the body of water must be fresh water.

2. It is true that old-world armies were guided by means of smoke and fire. But if we follow this phenomenon all the way through the book of Exodus it apparently was a special phenomenon granted to Israel. It cannot be explained as the carrying of burning torches or braziers and still do justice to the text.

3. The definitive study of *chesed* is that of Nelson Glueck, *Chesed in the Bible* (Cincinnati: The Hebrew Union College Press, 1967). It includes an introductory essay by Gerald Larue in which he brings up to date the studies about *chesed* since Glueck's first publication (1927).

strong covenant word. God maintains the covenant with man on this ground. It is inherent in the Greek agape—divine, forgiving, accepting, unmerited love.

The psalm ends with the words "The LORD will reign for ever and ever" (v. 18). The whole Exodus experience is a commentary on what the reign of God is. He reigns through the means which He uses: His judgment and salvation. The beginnings of the concept of the Kingdom of God are in the Old Testament. It is the concept of the Kingdom that unites the theories of salvation, church, and eschatology in the New Testament. We must be careful that we do not think of the reign of God only in terms of the future: either of the millennium or of heaven. The Kingdom of God has come, is coming and will come.

Notes

[illegible]

7
The God of Every Crisis
Exodus 15:22—18:27

The First Crisis of Survival—Water—Exodus 15:22-27

We are not given all the details of the flight out of Egypt. We know the Israelites took unleavened bread and we suppose that they took water. Water is heavy (about sixty-two pounds per cubic foot) and human beings use it in great quantities compared to food. So it would be water they would run out of first. Furthermore the territory that Israel was crossing, the Desert of Shur,[1] is not known for an abundance of water. Therefore we can understand the frustration of the Israelites when they came upon their first water supply at Marah and found it bitter (15:23).

When the people grumbled God showed Moses a tree and when the wood from the tree was plunged into the water, the water became sweet (v. 25). Travelers and pioneers know of such trees although no such tree now exists in the Sinaitic Peninsula. It is assumed that one did then, for the Lord did not pick out any tree but specified one with such powers. As in every miraculous occurrence in Exodus to this point, we find here something natural tinged with something supernatural.

Older interpreters liken this tree to the cross that sweetens the bitterness of our sin by divine forgiveness. It is a charming idea, but hardly the thought here or anywhere expressed in the New Testament. Others spiritualize it and say that God can sweeten the waters of the bitterness of human experience. Again it is a charming idea but not the point.

The point is that the God of salvation is also the God of providence! Whom God saves He cares for! Whom He loves He provides for. Water was needed; God provided for it.

The second supply of water was at Elim (15:27), apparently a natural oasis. Rain and snow fall on mountains hundreds of miles from an oasis. The water seeps downward from the slopes until it hits a bedrock formation. Then it follows this bedrock for hundreds of miles. Where the formation is faulted it comes to the surface. This is why oases appear magically in an ocean of sand or why wells can be dug in apparently waterless places. Finding water at Elim was a result of being providentially led by God in the long way around from Egypt to Palestine.

In between Marah and Elim God made an unusual announcement to Israel. He would be the Healer of Israel (15:26). Why does this section occur here? What is its context? It may be connected with the healing of the bitter water of Marah. God is saying in effect, "Just as I could heal the bitter waters of Marah I can heal your bitter diseases."

It may have been, on the other hand, a warning in transit. Perhaps Israel now thought that she was spiritually superior to the Egyptians. She was now "in good" with the Lord. But the Lord was saying that no relationship with

Him is automatic, neutral, without spiritual qualifications. Israel too could be plagued! She too could suffer from the diseases the Lord put on Egypt (15:26). Therefore a spiritual and obedient response was always required of Israel. Israel was to (a) diligently hearken to God's voice; (b) do that which is right in His eyes; (c) give heed to His commandments; and (d) keep all His statutes. Then God would be the Lord, their healer.

The application to Christian faith should be clear. True, we are saved, justified, regenerated by faith in Christ. As great as are the wonder and grace, the moral demands are not relaxed. Spirituality is demanded of saints in the New Testament as much as it was of Israelites in the Old. Grace is no neutral resting place but a place where righteousness seeks to prevail.

The Second Great Crisis—Food—Exodus 16:1-36

Because the Israelites left in haste they could carry little food. They had flocks and cattle but those would be consumed in time. Travelers figure on forty days' food to cross the peninsula with additional food for safety's sake. The Israelites had been on the march more than a month. As they moved into the Desert of Sin (no connection with our word "sin"!) which is generally in the southwest of the Sinaitic Peninsula they ran out of food. Hence they grumbled.

Again they declared that their state in Egypt was preferable to that of a free nation in a semiarid country. They longed for the Egyptian pots full of meat and bread they could eat to the full. This was most likely an exaggeration to embarrass Moses.

God promised quails in place of the meat and manna in

place of the bread. They would not banquet and glut on this diet but it would sustain them. God would not have saved His people from the Destroyer at midnight and later from the army of Pharaoh only to let them starve to death in the Desert of Sin.

As with everything in the Exodus, the story of the rain of bread from heaven blends the natural with the supernatural. There are a number of possible sources of a substance like manna. Most scholars prefer to think it was a substance oozed by insects that live in the tamarisk tree. "From heaven" means that at night it fell from the trees onto the ground. Here again there is some basis for the supernatural, the supply of manna in the natural order. But the amount of it, the fact that it followed the Israelites for forty years and its peculiar qualities mean that none of the substances suggested as manna can meet all these qualifications. Whatever natural substance it might have been it needed an extra boost from the supernatural so that it could be the daily bread for Israel for forty years.

Quails migrate from Arabia and North Africa to southern Europe. After long flights they fly low or they rest in the sand and may easily be beaned! They can be cured and kept for a period of time. Again the natural is touched with just enough of the supernatural so that the supply of meat never failed the Israelites.

Although there is not space to discuss this long chapter in detail, certain theological and practical matters may be noted:

1. We see more of the fulfillment of the God who "will be what He will be." He would reveal His nature in the ongoing of history. His love and providence were here revealed in supplying the manna and the quails.

2. The manna was to be gathered according to rules

and according to strict Sabbath observation. Even in respect to eating there may be moral involvement. Here was a test of Israel's faith and obedience: Would they trust the providence of God and would they keep the rules? That God is a moral God had to be stipulated in such materialistic terms for Israel was learning her moral ABC's.

3. The manna was to kept as a testimony that was to be put in the ark in the Tabernacle (16:31-36). This was done in accordance with the biblical view of history that God's great deeds of the past have significance for every generation. It is a sign and reminder of the providence of God: that when Israel was about to perish for hunger, God graciously supplied them with bread.

4. We gain some insights into the structure of God's providence in the supply of the quails and the manna. As we have said repeatedly in the exodus events we have the natural with a tinge of the supernatural. Providence in our lives is such a mixture. Christians who are always being directed by God every moment of every day overplay the supernatural. Those who simply identify the natural order with providence overplay the natural. That we may entertain angels unaware should warn us that we should never so frame the doctrine of providence so as to eliminate a tinge of the supernatural.

Yet this is a matter of faith. No man can write out a formula for the relationship of the natural and the supernatural. God supplies our daily bread through sun, rain, farmers, bakers, truck drivers and markets. Yet there may be times that our bread comes to us unexpectedly through a very special providence of God. Faith hesitates to tinge all with the supernatural for the natural is also an instrument of God; and faith hesitates to rationalize providence in such a way that all that is is providential.

5. Our Lord is called manna from heaven. "This is the bread that came down from heaven. Our forefathers ate manna and died but he who feeds on this bread will live forever" (John 6:58). Bread is a side dish in America but for millions in the Near East, Middle East and Europe it was a substantial part of a meal. It was not overrefined as is our bread in America. The typology of manna is here set out as that substantial Bread who through the Incarnation came down from heaven. Faith in this bread leads to life everlasting.

Again Water! Again Grumbling! Again Supply!—Exodus 17:1-17

The first seven verses of chapter 17 bring a reenactment of a now familiar drama: Israel faces another crisis of survival; Israel complains bitterly to Moses; God again provides for their needs.

The Israelites could not make long marches but moved by stages, i.e., so many miles a day with a camp at the end of each period of marching. This would greatly consume water so that when they reached Rephidim[2] ("resting places") they were out of water.

As usual the Israelites grumbled and as usual they said it would be better to be in Egypt than to be killed by thirst. No doubt thirst can kill!

Moses apparently had gained much faith for he thought that the people's response was an unnecessary tempting of God's power to provide. Then at the injunction of the Lord, Moses took some elders with him and struck a rock in Horeb and water came out of the rock. The people and their cattle could drink and they would not die in the Desert of Sin.

There are other stories of rocks being struck in these

mountains and of water coming out. One commentator mentions a Sudanese camel corps that tracked down the source of dripping water. They hit the face of the cliff which they had exposed and a stream of water gushed out.

Here again we have the natural tinged with the supernatural. No one at that time knew enough about such rock formations to accomplish the feat of drawing water from rock. True, Moses had been around these parts, but he appeared in the text to be ignorant of the phenomenon. Only under the direction of Yahweh did he find water.

The immediate message is: once again God expresses His providence towards Israel. The theme is becoming familiar. The God who saves, keeps; the God who redeems, preserves; the God who delivers, provides! The God and Father of our Lord Jesus Christ who justified us at the moment of faith is the God and Father of the sparrow that falls, of the hairs of our head, of our daily bread, of our prayers that are an asking, seeking and knocking.

Paul speaks of the journey of the Israelites in 1 Corinthians 10:1-6. In passing he wrote: "They drank from the spiritual rock that accompanied them, and that rock was Christ" (10:4). The identification of Christ with manna, with the smitten rock and with the water of life (John 4:10-15) shows how deeply the New Testament takes the typology of the exodus experiences of Israel. So Christ is to the Christian that "spiritual rock" that is the source of the continual renewal of strength whereby he lives the Christian life.

After Hunger and Thirst, War—Exodus 17:8-16

In this passage Israel faces another crisis: war. The Amalekites (cousins of Israel) roamed as bedouins or semibedouins deep down into the Sinaitic Peninsula. They were apprehensive of Israel's coming there because it was part of their "bread basket" and any such large numbers of foreigners were a military threat.

To protect themselves they began by attacking the most defenseless of the Israelites—the stragglers (see Deut. 25:17). Moses knew his only recourse was battle. He appointed Joshua to select out his fighting men and to go to battle with the Amalekites. The Israelites had left Egypt properly armed (see Exod. 13:18). Joshua was successful for he "overcame the Amalekite army with the sword" (17:13).

There was another aspect to the battle. Moses went up to a place where he had a "stadium seat" to view the battle. With him were Aaron and Hur, the latter apparently being a prominent member of the council of the elders. When Moses held up his hands with the rod of the Lord the Israelites prevailed; when his hands dropped, Amalek prevailed. Moses was perhaps too old to fight or fighting wasn't his specialty. At any rate, it was a very tiring stance so he had to sit down and have Aaron and Hur hold his hands up. What did this mean?

1. Certainly it wasn't for the psychological effect. That is, when the Israelites looked up and saw the rod of the Lord with perhaps the Israelite banner on it they took courage and fought; when they did not see it they became discouraged and fell back. This would trivialize the whole scene on the mountain.

2. The more traditional explanation is that Moses' hands were lifted up in prayer. This is reading back into the record too much of our own twentieth-century piety. Further, it does not explain the concluding verses of the passage.

3. To us the obvious meaning is that just as God provided water and bread in the wilderness to the Israelites He could also provide protection for them from the attack of Israel's enemies. The rod was the instrument by which all things were accomplished by the power of God. It meant then that Israel won by virtue of the power of God and not by her own strength or military cunning. This is behind the whole theory of war in Israel.

The moral is that just as Israel was dependent on the Lord for deliverance from Egypt, for crossing the Red Sea, for bread and for water, so Israel was dependent on the Lord for her battles. The rod of the Lord was the sign that it was God's strength, God's power and God's enablement that brought victory. When the rod drooped it meant that Israel was fighting with her own strength and could not prevail.

The lesson to the Christian should be obvious. No more than Israel can we win our own conflicts in our own strength. Our strength and our wisdom must come from God.

But again we have the natural tinged with the supernatural. Israel had to fight (the natural) but could win only by virtue of the rod of God (the supernatural). How difficult for Christians to find this happy balance! Yet how true it is for Christians as it was for Israel.

War was a way of life in that ancient world and it was also true of Israel. Two things separate Israel's view of war from other views. First, the goal of war and of all political life was peace—*shalom*. Shalom was not merely a "cease-fire," a truce, a treaty, but a state of positive, healthy, wholesome reconciliation with one's enemies. Second, Israel never had a holy war in the Moslem sense of spreading one's faith. Her wars were defensive wars for her protection. Her concept of war degenerated as she became increasingly a power in the ancient Near East world.

War was "holy" in Israel in that (a) all of her institutions were holy because Israel was a theocracy and this must include the way she went to war; (b) the victory was always the Lord's victory; the chief and best way of winning being the Lord terrifying the enemy so that they fled with no shedding of blood; and (c) the basic attitude of the Israelite soldier was belief in the power of Yahweh, not the courage of battle.

The concluding two verses suggest that the meaning of Moses' uplifted hands and the rod of God is that the victory is of the Lord. The rod was not a psychological stimulus to the warriors nor was Moses' praying. "The LORD is my banner" (17:15) means that the banner that Israel's armies carried into battle was not a literal banner but the Lord. The Lord was the sign of Israel's victory. The altar Moses built was a memorial to the fact that the Lord gave the victory against the Amalekites.

Jethro Learns Something and Teaches Something—Exodus 18:1-27

The news of Israel had circulated so widely in that region that Jethro knew that Israel had come out of Egypt, that Israel was near Mount Sinai and that Moses was the leader. So he came to pay his respects and brought Moses' wife and two children.

On the surface, chapter 18 is a charming story of two old friends who had lived together for forty years when Moses was in Midian. They greet each other in peace, have a friendly talk, have a meal together before God, talk over the problem of administering justice and part in peace.

There are some deeper elements to the chapter. Certainly one reason for the chapter is to hear the confession of Jethro: "Now I know that the LORD is greater than all other gods" (v. 11). The people of that cultural epoch saw such struggles rightly, viewing them as conflicts of principalities and powers, i.e., among the gods. That Israel escaped from Egypt was a clear sign that the Lord of the Israelites was greater than the gods of Egypt.

This was the first great contest in that ancient world between a polytheistic faith of many gods and monotheistic faith of one God. In this contest, Yahweh the God of Israel, the Maker of heaven and earth, clearly showed that He is the one, only true and living God. The importance of this account of Jethro is that it shows that other peoples recognized this.

There is also the willingness of Jethro spiritually to identify himself with Israel and the elders of Israel in return. Jethro offered up two sacrifices of thanksgiving to Yahweh and ate a sacrificial meal with Moses, Aaron and the elders of Israel "in the presence of God" (v. 12). This has led to speculation that Moses learned much of his knowledge of Yahweh, sacrifices and practical law from his years in Midian with Jethro.

Some scholars attribute little or nothing to Jethro and the Kenites. Others are elaborate in their speculations that the true Yahweh concept and worship was given by Jethro and the Kenites to Moses and then to Israel. Perhaps the truth here is that the account shows the measure of the true knowledge of God among all the descendants of Abraham.

The second part of the chapter concerns the advice

Jethro gave to Moses about handling his large case load of disputes. We see here two important items: (a) Something of Moses' training in the house of Pharaoh manifested itself in his handling of cases at law; and (b) the Israelites judged Moses to be a charismatic person who by virtue of his close union with God would know the right judgment. All the judges, warriors and kings of Israel were expected to be charismatic persons. That is the nature of the case in a theocracy. God's Spirit is the immediate source of power, virtue and wisdom.

In picking out men to handle the lesser cases Moses was to follow substantial criteria. These men too were to be men of the Spirit. It is much the same in the book of Acts. The newly appointed deacons had to have a human qualification (wisdom) and a divine qualification ("full of the Spirit," Acts 6:3). What better advice can we give today for the Lord's servants than that they get wisdom through the best education they can get and at the same time be charismatically endowed by being men of the Spirit?

Although some scholars think that following Jethro's advice was a mistake on Moses' part, the text offers no such assessment. In fact the advice appears like an act of kindness to an overworked man who couldn't quite see how to ease the burden.

Notes

1. Because the Exodus occurred so long ago the geographical sites are very difficult to locate. The Desert of Shur is the northwest part of Sinai. Shur is thought to come from the word "wall," hence where the walls or fortresses were built to protect Egypt from armies coming down the coast.

Marah is tentatively identified with Ain Hawarah and Elim with Wadi Gharandel.

2. Again geographical sites are difficult to identify although every yard of the Sinaitic Peninsula has been checked. Rephidim has been tentatively identified as Wadi (a wash) Refayid or perhaps Wadi Feiran.

8
A Law We Can Live By
Exodus 19:1—24:11

The Tribes Become a Nation: the Covenant Offered and Accepted—Exodus 19:1-8

Moses kept the log. He mentioned the date—three months after the Exodus; he mentioned the place—the Desert of Sinai; he mentioned the spot—before the mountain. The traditional site is Jebel Musa, Mountain of Moses, which juts up 7,500 feet.

Up to this point Israel had been held together spiritually by the terms given to Abraham and binding on all his descendants; and as a people by a federation of tribes held together by a council of elders. At Sinai they were to come under the detailed covenant of the Law; and they were to be forged into a nation—a theocracy which is a nation "under God."

It is Paul who is most specific about the relationship of the covenant made at Sinai and the New Covenant in Jesus Christ, both in Romans and Galatians. The book of Hebrews also treats this theme. These Epistles help us to understand the New Testament attitude toward the relationship of the covenant sealed in Exodus 24 and the New Covenant in Christ.

Certain important matters appear in these eight verses:

1. *The basis of the covenant.* The basis of the covenant was divine redemption: "I carried you on eagles' wings and brought you to myself" (19:4). This is a touching image. The mother bird sweeps under the young eagle as it is learning to fly and bears it up if it isn't making it. So as a compassionate mother, God tenderly bore Israel out of Egypt to the nest at Mount Sinai.

There is another tender note in the expression "to myself." This speaks of the very real "existential" relationship between Israel and Yahweh. It anticipates His fatherly relationship in the New Testament to Christians who are owned as sons by the God and Father of our Lord Jesus Christ.

2. *The reward of the covenant.* Exodus 19:5,6 is really "what it's all about!" Right from the beginning of the book God wanted Israel for a unique treasure, a kingdom of priests and a holy nation. These were marvelous benedictions for Israel.

A treasure or a special possession is something all people are familiar with. How carefully we guard our family heirlooms or antiques! How greatly a collector cherishes his stamps or his coins or his books! How much concern we give to guarding our jewelry, especially when it has sentimental value. So Israel was God's very valuable "family possession."

Israel was also a kingdom of priests. This means that before God, every Israelite had been redeemed to a special status. Even though later on Israel would be given priests, that could not detract from the fact that in view of the exodus event of redemption every Israelite stood in relationship to God different from all other nations.

Israel was a holy nation. Note carefully: *Israel was now called a nation.* As a nation she was a holy nation. She was holy because she belonged to God through the exodus redemption. She was holy because she would be given a list of holy things—sacrifices, a priesthood, a Temple, prophets, kings and a Book.

That Israel was a special possession (a treasure), a kingdom of priests and a holy nation is set within the context of the nations of all the earth. The Lord said: "The whole earth is mine" (19:5). That means that all the nations or tribes of the world are under the lordship of Yahweh. Israel was not raising its "god" to universal significance; rather the God of all nations was raising Israel to universal significance. If Yahweh were a tribal god or purely the God of one nation He would not interest us. To the contrary, these events on the Sinaitic Peninsula concerned the God of all the world, all its tribes, all its nations and all its kingdoms.

There is something deeply typological in these three characteristics of Israel. Peter applies them to the church (see 1 Pet. 2:5-9). That which is said of Israel is not a shadow but a reality; but it does "shadow forth" another reality. That reality is the Christian church of the New Testament. This means that these exodus events embody a great typology—and again we mean typology in the most comprehensive sense of a very special kind of history and not in the narrower sense of a type with its antitype or fulfillment. These events anticipate a continuous people of God that is universal and worldwide in distribution—the Christian church.

3. *The terms of the covenant.* The covenant demanded obedience from Israel and the keeping of its terms. Having such conditional terms, it was not a covenant of pure

grace. However, it is the message of the New Testament that there must be a covenant of this nature in order for man to understand the covenant of pure grace in Christ.

On the positive side, this covenant said something that the covenant of grace also says. God's relationships with man are never neutral, i.e., free from the moral imperative. God is always careful to inform man that man's relationship to Him, no matter how gracious, is always morally structured. Grace is as much a summons to righteousness as is law.

When the people heard the terms of the covenant they accepted them. "We will do everything the LORD has said" (19:8). Because Israel so responded, God followed through with the terms of the covenant (chapters 20—23) and then with the ratification of the covenant (chapter 24).

Yahweh and Israel Meet to Hear the Terms Of the Covenant—Exodus 19:9-25

Israel had heard the invitation to make a covenant with Moses and had replied in the affirmative. God took them at their word and gave Moses instructions concerning how He would approach Israel and announce the terms of the covenant:

1. *God would come down.* When a covenant is made the parties must meet! God is in His heaven and man is on earth. Man cannot ascend to heaven but God can come to earth. So God said that He would come down to where Israel was, to spell out the terms of the covenant. The entire mountain was to be turned into a great temple and temple area for this majestic encounter. Hence twice in the account God said that He would come down (19:9,11). This is the heart of the whole biblical concept of revela-

tion: God comes to man! The Shepherd finds the sheep! The great quest for God is the divine quest for man!

2. *The people must consecrate themselves.* There is a protocol when people are introduced to royalty. Certain things are specified (e.g., the kinds of clothing that are acceptable) and other things are assumed (that one has washed, shaved, combed the hair). In meeting God the protocol calls for sanctification.

To prepare for God's coming to them meant that the people were to wash their clothes from all earthly defilement. The men were to refrain from sexual intercourse (19:15), perhaps not so much from any sense of defilement as in the sense of conserving physical and psychological energies in preparation for the appearance of God. Finally, they were to keep their place and not trespass the mountain which had become a temple of God for the giving of the terms of the covenant.

3. *The Lord would come down "in the sight of all the people"* (v. 11). God is an invisible Spirit, however, and cannot be seen by the human eye. His presence is known through signs in the cosmos that man can interpret only as caused by the presence of God. This is what is meant by a theophany—a manifestation of God perceptible to man's senses.

To give a sense of the greatness of this theophany we set out the items related to it in serial order: thunder, lightning, thick cloud, trumpet blast, Mount Sinai wrapped in smoke, fire, the whole mountain trembled greatly. What Israelite could doubt God was there?

So God was on the mountain; the people were gathered before it. The terms of the covenant could be pronounced as the covenantal partners were now face-to-face.

The New Testament addresses itself to this scene (see Heb. 12:18-24). It says that the covenant of grace in Jesus Christ is not this terrifying scene. This is law in its power to frighten in its suggestion of terrible judgment! Christians come to God too! The record says: "But you have come to Mount Zion, and to the heavenly Jerusalem, the city of the living God. You have come to thousands upon thousands of angels in joyful assembly, to the church of the firstborn, whose names are written in heaven. You have come to God, the judge of all men, to the spirits of righteous men made perfect, to Jesus the mediator of a new covenant, and to the sprinkled blood that speaks a better word than the blood of Abel" (12:22-24).

What is the fundamental difference in this connection between church and synagogue? The synagogue considers the covenant made at Sinai *eternal*. This is the last and final covenant of God.

The Church has said that this is a great covenant. But there is yet one more covenant: the New Covenant. This is our Lord's stance when He established Holy Communion as the sacred meal and memorial of the New Covenant sealed in His blood. This is the stance of Paul in Romans and Galatians where he argues the limited nature of the covenant of law and asserts that the covenant of grace is the *eternal* covenant made with Abraham and renewed and enlarged in Jesus Christ. This is the stance of the letter to the Hebrews which sees the covenant of the law fulfilled and replaced by the New Covenant in Christ.

There are many things at stake in the contrast between law and grace. We pick out just one: *universality*. The covenant made with Abraham was in principle universal. He is the great archetype of those justified by faith. Hence the New Testament makes much of Abraham. But the law is a limited, national covenant. Moses is not the father of us all. The law was a preliminary, instructional, typological, disciplinary, national covenant. It was never meant to be universal. Only the people of God as a series of congregations (churches) can be universal; only a covenant of grace can be universal; and only the covenant made with the universal Man, Jesus Christ, can be universal.

The Ten Words of the Terms of the Covenant—Exodus 20:1-20

The God who redeems a people from Egypt expects such redeemed people to be a moral people. Redemption comes first, then morality. But the sequence must be followed: if redeemed, then moral.

The concept of God as a God of indefectible morality had not been declared as yet. It had been implied in such expressions as "Who is like you—majestic in holiness" (15:11) and as He has a "holy dwelling" (15:13). Further, the notion that the plagues were judgments suggested the holiness of God for a judgment is based on divine, moral rectitude.

With the giving of the Ten Commandments and the ordinances it now clearly established that Yahweh is a righteous, holy, moral God.

The intent of the Ten Commandments and the ordinances is that the redeemed people also be moral people, just people, people who pursue equity in all social relationships. The great biblical theme that the worshipers of a holy God must themselves pursue holiness is stated in Leviticus 11:45: "I am the LORD who brought you up out of Egypt to be your God; therefore be holy, because I am holy" (a concept echoed in 1 Pet. 1:16).

The scriptural doctrine of grace and of man's depravity

means that redemption must precede morality. The Exodus must come before the Ten Commandments. Salvation leads, morality follows.

To have morality precede salvation is salvation by works. To mix salvation with works is the Galatian heresy of mixing grace and law, Christ and Moses, the cross and the commandments, faith and obedience.

Those who own up to Christ also must own up to morality. Those who claim to be born of the Spirit must walk in the Spirit. We who have been saved by grace come under the severest moral mandate: "We died to sin; how can we live in it any longer?" (Rom. 6:2).

That the commandments number ten is a biblical declaration (Exod. 34:28, Deut. 4:13, 10:4). The expression in the Hebrew language is Ten Words. A "word" in this context means a royal edict, the mandate of a king. Hence with reference to God it means an edict, mandate or proclamation of God. Or it may be paraphrased: "God's Word on this subject."

The influence of the Ten Words on Western morality and law is beyond calculation. They have come to be recognized as the basis of all public morality. In law they were considered the basis of common law; legal codes of the Middle Ages were usually prefaced by the Ten Commandments. Some theologians have proposed that the Ten Commandments were written on the heart of Adam and others that they are the embodiment and reiteration of the natural law, the moral light of reason (cf. Rom. 2:14,15).

Although the Scriptures state that there are Ten Words, nowhere does it number them. As a result, several different numbering systems have arisen. If the prologue (20:1,2) is counted as the first commandment it alters the count. Commentators are agreed that the precise numbering is immaterial in comparison to the content of the passage.

The most natural background for understanding the Ten Commandments is the typical old-world suzerainty treaty (the sovereign lord with the humble vassal). (a) The lord or king identifies himself; (b) he lists all the benefits he has bestowed on his vassal in the past; (c) the bulk of the treaty is then the listing of the obligations; (d) loyalty to the lord by the vassal is demanded with a ban upon any foreign alliances; (e) a list of cursings and blessings is given; (f) the treaty is put "on deposit" in a temple in the two countries involved so that the gods may inspect them; (g) the treaty may be continuously renewed (see Deut. 5); (h) a list of the divine witnesses is given; and (i) the treaty is sealed, usually by some sort of ritual like a sacrifice. The Hebrew expression to make a covenant is "to cut a covenant" and suggests a sacrifice. Obviously the parallels of such a suzerainty treaty and the entire Sinaitic revelation (Exod. 19—24) are numerous and some very close.

Apart from the teaching of each commandment, or word, there are certain features that govern the entirety of them:

1. The covenantal terms and their moral element are based on redemption (20:2, see also 19:4). God's saving and delivering of Israel is again put in the form of the beautiful metaphor of a mother eagle bearing up her fledglings.

2. These laws have a universal character. They are not based on a local custom, a local bit of geography and so on. Nor are they culturally and historically bound but they are applicable to all places and all times where man is found. Nor are they nationalistic but they apply to human nature universally—they are transcultural.

3. They are simple, absolute and programmatic asser-

tions. They are the kind of programmatic statements that rest behind all specific law. They are not divided up into possible cases (that comes later) for they are stating rather the spirit, the character, the pattern of morality. All individual precepts derive from that.

4. They are without parallel. When the codes of nations predating Israel's were discovered, it was said at first that Israel's codes were just more of the same. More mature analysis has shown how far superior the law of Israel was and is. There is no parallel to the Ten Words in Confucianism, Buddhism, Zoroastrianism, Islam or the ancient religion of Egypt.

5. The "you shall not" of many of the commandments sounds restrictive and negative. Should not ethics be positive and affirmative? Not quite so! What is not prohibited is permitted. An affirmative statement tends to be universalistic in nature. Which of us can sort out all the possibilities in a statement that is universal in scope? None! But with a prohibition all things outside the prohibition may be possible. So actually the "you shall not" character of the commandments is freer than it seems on first reading.

6. One of the reasons we in the Christian world know of the Ten Commandments and only scholars know of the Sumerian, Accadian, Hittite and Middle Assyrian laws and the famous Code of Hammurabi is the pure monotheism of the Ten Words. Even if it be argued that pure monotheism is not explicitly taught in "you shall have no other gods before me" (20:3) the thrust, the spirit of the Ten Words is certainly in that direction. Or put conversely, no gross polytheism nor old-world mythology exists in the Ten Commandments.

7. One of the greatest messages of the Ten Words is that it is impossible from a biblical perspective to separate

morality (or ethics) from religion.

In philosophy in the past one hundred years one of the most marked efforts which is still powerful today has been the effort to separate ethics from religion. This view affirms that ethics or morality can be developed purely on its own presuppositions and does not need any assist from, let alone basis in, religion. The very structure of the Ten Words forbids this.

The Ten Words divide into four commandments about man's conception and worship of God and into six about man's relationship to man. Unfortunately, in so many discussions of the Ten Commandments in ethics, the first four are omitted or passed over so that the emphasis falls on the last six. This is a betrayal of the Ten Words.

According to the Ten Commandments to be moral one must first be redeemed—we mean moral in the full biblical sense of morality, not that non-Christian men are not moral. Further, to be moral one must be in covenantal relationship with God. *The Ten Commandments are not a pure piece of ethics but are terms of a covenant between man and God.* They can be understood and kept only in a covenantal, i.e., religious or spiritual context. Therefore how a man thinks of God, redemption and covenant is basic to biblical ethics. A nonreligious ethics in this sense would be preposterous.

We live now in the day of statism. Modern states are not rooted in religious faith. They operate in the realm of law very pragmatically and functionally. This means the state determines that which is right or wrong. *That means man prescribes his own morality; there is no higher court of appeal.* If the state has a large heritage of good will the result is not too bad. But when a state has more sinister intentions as did Germany under Hitler and Russia under

Stalin, it can commit terrible atrocities and murder in the name of justice as decreed by the state. *If ethics rises out of religion, then such action is impossible.* All dictators and states are responsible to a higher law than that which man decrees for himself.

Warnings About Worship—Exodus 20:21-26

When Israel left Mount Sinai she would encounter many of the pagan peoples of that region. All of these peoples had their religions, their altars, their temples and their sacrifices. There was a strong possibility that Israel would uncritically imitate the practices of some of these pagan tribes and corrupt her own true worship of the one, living God. Therefore prohibitions to guard against such possible infiltration are given in Exodus 20:21-26, disconnected as they may seem in the narrative.

First, the Israelites were to be very careful not to fall into idolatry. It was one thing not to make their own graven images (20:4-6), but it might be another to escape being fascinated by the beautiful gold and silver idols of other peoples (v. 23).

Second, they were to be sure that they had the proper altar. It was not to be one hewn with metal but the rocks were to be used in their natural state. Although we do not know the specific wrong involved here we do know that the command was intended to ward off some pagan method of worship as in verse 26. It may be that the weapons of war were not to be used for the altar of God. It may mean that rocks in their natural state are "of God" but carved up are "of man."

Third, the altar was not to be a high one with steps like those found in Petra and Megiddo. Nakedness of the priests—as practiced by some in that ancient world—or exposure of the priest was forbidden by the holy God of Israel (v. 26).

Specific Ordinances in Contrast to Programmatic Law—Exodus 21:1—23:33

The Ten Commandments are simple, comprehensive, religious and moral principles. In contrast there is the wretchedly complex character of human life. Is all killing murder? Are all sexual irregularities of the same seriousness? To bridge the gulf between the simple absolutes of the Ten Commandments and complexity of everyday life we have the book of the Covenant (24:7).

Although we believe that the end product is eventually a matter of divine revelation, there is some human precedent for the various rules. Again we mention Moses' forty years in the court of Pharaoh. We do not know but can only speculate that he must have learned some practical law there. Further, he spent forty years in Midian where he certainly learned much of tribal, common law. As we learned from his experience with Jethro in chapter 18 he had already been carrying on his own court of common law.

Chapter 21 commences with the "laws" (v. 1) or "judgments" or "legal rulings" or "social laws"—as they have been variously called. These are culturally and historically bound to a certain period of Israel's history and to a certain cultural backdrop. It is therefore of not too great profit to comment on law after law. However, laws are specific incarnations of the justice of God and we can learn from them.

1. In that God's people are to be holy, merciful and just, their lives and social relationships are to express these virtues. The very general commandments of the

Ten Commandments must be given specific interpretation that reflects the nature of the Ten Commandments. Or to put it another way, general attitudes of justice, mercy and holiness must be expressed in specifics in the experiences of daily life.

2. We must not be surprised by some of the rules that seem odd to us. There is a large historical and cultural gap between ancient Israel and modern North America. People can exist only within the framework of a culture. In this sense all peoples of all times and all geographical locations are limited by their culture. Our modern culture is not a universal, transcultural culture! One's culture is reflected in one's laws. There were slaves in that old-world culture. So Israel, being part of that culture, needed laws about slaves.

Before we write off many of these ordinances as crude or pre-Christian we must face the reality that all human beings exist only in culture situations. The more transcultural a moral prescript is the more general it must become. Cultural rules for specific cultures must be very specific. In being so specific they are not always appreciated by people in a very different culture. One basic moral maxim will be incarnated a thousand different ways in a thousand different cultures.

3. Laws that seem cruel or inhuman to us do not appear so when the cultural context is better understood. There is a rule that appears odd to us about beating a slave. If the slave is killed the owner is guilty of his death. But if the slave lives a day or so there is no penalty. Even being guilty of his death is not being guilty of the death penalty but of some stipulated penalty—"since the slave is his property" (21:21).

Of course there are answers or explanations for each

of these particular rules. However, we need a wider perspective. If we understand the nature of life and culture reflected in this ancient legislation we will see that such rules are not so cruel as we are wont to think. We may see things askew if we judge them solely from our cultural perspective and not take the time to learn something of that cultural epoch.

4. A basic sense of justice and humanitarianism can be seen running through these ordinances. The Ten Commandments forbid murder. There are cases when there is no intent to kill. In 21:12,14 a distinction is made between murder and the accidental killing of a man. A man who is guilty of manslaughter flees to a city of refuge. This kind of practice would be necessary until there was a more sophisticated system of courts. It meant that the full penalty of the law was not to crush a man who accidentally killed another man.

There is a law against kidnapping (21:16). This means that to destroy a man's liberty and peril his life is as terrible as murder. Such a law is possible only as one sees its ultimate ground as the sacredness of the person.

5. The ordinances show a sensitivity about the perversion of justice. That there should be no bearing of false witness is to assure the integrity of the court. The court can only serve justice when it is sustained by truth. To allow false witnesses is to destroy truth, which is to destroy justice, which is to destroy the court.

A good man may team up with a bad man *for the good man's own profit.* This furthers the career of the evil man so the ordinances forbid it (23:1). Most men lose their sense of moral integrity when under the influence of a mob. Mobs, then, can pervert justice by destroying the moral integrity of individuals. Therefore it is forbidden to join a mob so as to pervert justice (23:2).

The poor present a particular problem. We may pity a poor man because he is poor and overlook his wickedness. This should not be done (23:3). But the poor may be intimidated because he is poor. This too ought not to be done (23:6).

Perhaps as soon as courts emerged in man's civilizing process, the taking of bribes emerged. Acceptance of bribes has always been the dirty linen of the legal profession. There is a stern law against yielding to bribery (23:8).

6. One of the mandates of justice is that a man should conduct his affairs so as not to injure other people. A man cannot dig a pit and leave it unprotected. If an animal falls into the pit and is injured or killed the man who dug the pit is liable (21:33,34). Swimming pools, gravel pits and discarded refrigerators still kill our children. Throughout the text here is the belief that no man is an island.

There cannot be the willy-nilly killing of a thief. A thief may be killed at night but not in the daytime. Today many states make a similar distinction. Burglary at night may carry a mandatory imprisonment of five years; burglary during the daytime may have a much lesser penalty (unless the person is armed with a deadly weapon). Again the power of the law to crush as well as penalize is moderated.

7. The backdrop of some of these laws is the love for one's neighbor. "When he cries out to me [God], I will hear, *for I am compassionate*" (22:27, italics added). God's faithful love to Israel is called *chesed.* Each Israelite is to reflect this divine *chesed* in his own life in the manner in which he treats his neighbor. For example, the responsible manner in which a man treats a borrowed animal reflects

his love towards his neighbor (22:14,15).

Love for a neighbor comes out very clearly in the ordinances about a stranger. Strangers who are at a disadvantage in a community are not to be wronged (22:21).

There is a law against interest (22:25-27). This also reflects love to one's neighbor. In an agrarian culture, money is a scarce item. Repaying the capital of a loan is burden enough. The addition of interest may make it an unbearable burden. Further, a garment taken as surety is to be returned at night so the owner will not sleep cold. If an owner cries in the night because he is cold, God will hear him (22:27).

Another facet of love for a neighbor involves the treatment of the straying animal of an enemy. The Israelite is to act as responsibly in this situation as towards a friend (23:4,5).

8. Because Israel is a people of God, there are also religious ordinances. A study of the laws of other peoples of that old world shows that as far as can be discerned their laws were purely pragmatic. They had no divine basis. Only in Israel is there the very close association of the divine Majesty and human ordinances. As we saw in the Ten Commandments, one cannot separate religion and ethics. So it is with the ordinances.

Any effort to bypass, through sorcery, God's prophetic order of giving His Word is a capital crime (22:18). Sacrificing to other gods was also a capital crime (22:20). The heathen custom of boiling a kid in its mother's milk is forbidden (23:19). Israel was to make no covenants with other gods (23:32).

Religious laws seem more and more obsolete to contemporary society. That is because contemporary society is increasingly secular whereas Israel was a theocracy. In

Israel all of life was under the rule and lordship of God. There had to be religious laws as well as civil laws in a theocracy so conceived.

The Christian thinks the same way. He worships the God and Father of our Lord Jesus Christ (redemption) and the God the Maker of all (creation). Under such universal lordship man's ethical concerns are religious as well as civil. A world view that is so intensely theocentric can think no other way.

The Covenant Is Ratified—Exodus 24:1-11

The great event in chapter 24 is the climax of the book of Exodus. Abraham's children were now a multitude the size of a nation. They were now to be bound into a covenantal relationship with God and forged into a nation—a theocracy or nation ruled over by God. With the ratification of the covenant they became in fact the great possession of Yahweh, a royal priesthood and a holy nation.

This scene is also prophetic. The New Testament uses it as the prototype of the ratification of the New Covenant in Christ (see Hebrews 9 and 10). There are many covenants made in the Old Testament but this one is singled out as the basic schema for the explanation of the New Covenant. It must be examined with the greatest seriousness. The following elements join the formation of the two covenants:

1. Moses was the mediator of the covenant. Even though the seventy elders went up to the mountain with Moses, it says in the text that "Moses alone is to approach the LORD" (24:2). A mediator is a go-between for two parties. He officially represents each to the other. Moses was Israel's man to God, and God's man to Israel.

One of the great themes of the New Testament is that

Christ is the Mediator of the New Covenant. As the Son of God incarnate He is God's representative to man; as the second Adam and the second Moses He is man's representative to God. He is the second Moses (see Heb. 3:1-6).

2. The covenant was made with the whole people of Israel. This fact is represented in different ways. Moses went up the mountain with Aaron, Nadab, Abihu and the seventy elders (24:1). When the altar was built at the base of the mountain, twelve pillars were erected to represent all of Israel (v. 4). When the book of the Covenant was read, all the people assented to its terms (v. 7).

This corporate character of the people of God runs through all of Scripture. The concepts of seed, heirs, tribe and nation are corporate terms. The New Testament word for church, *ecclesia,* is a corporate word, for it means an assembly or a congregation. Other corporate expressions in the New Testament are the church as a body, as a temple of the Spirit and as the bride of Christ.

The New Covenant is not strictly a personal covenant although people come under its terms one by one as persons. It is a covenant with the whole company of the redeemed. It is the new humanity, the new race made in the image of Christ the second Adam.

3. This covenant was sealed with (a) a holy meal and (b) a holy sacrifice. Eating a meal is not only a means of refueling the body's supply of energy and chemicals but it is a social experience. A meal is usually partaken by a special group of people such as a family, a club, an association or a group of friends. A meal is part of the celebration of such events as a wedding, or an anniversary or a special occasion. In the ancient world it also had a profound religious meaning.

Galatians 2:11-14 reflects this. Eating with the Gentiles or not eating with them was to express a theological point! Paul had to correct Peter's theology by calling his attention to the theological implications of his eating policy!

In the old world there was a sacred meal. The relationship of God and man was expressed in a meal in which God and man participated. The seventy elders had a sacred meal with Yahweh as part of the way in which the covenant was sealed and ratified. They "saw God, and they ate and drank" (24:11). Along with sacrifices, this is the strongest way that ancient culture could express the unity of God and man, the harmony of God and man, in a covenantal relationship.

It requires one step of the imagination to see the Lord's Supper, Holy Communion or the Eucharist as a sacred meal in which God and man express their covenantal relationship in the New Covenant in the blood of Jesus Christ.

The second way the covenant was sealed was by the young men functioning as priests to sacrifice animals (v. 5). Moses divided the blood, throwing half against the altar and the other half towards the people—perhaps on the twelve pillars representing the people.

That sacrifice was the most profound of religious ceremonies in that ancient world. However, there is much difference of opinion about what a sacrifice meant. Some scholars think it is the notion of a perfect gift surrendered irrevocably to God by killing the animal. Others think that the blood was considered the most precious part of the animal so the blood of the animal had to be drawn. Others think that as life is released by death, so the blood, the carrier of life, must be shed to release the life. Others think the sacrifices are propitiatory of the divine holiness.

Hebrews 9:22 does give us some hint. It says that all things in the Tabernacle were purified by blood. But what does purified mean? In this verse, it stands for the forgiveness of sins. Perhaps the idea of sacrifice combines the notion of a perfect gift surrendered to God and a life surrendered as a propitiatory sacrifice so that the sins of the people would not prevent the formation of the covenantal pact.

Again the theme of Hebrews 9 and 10 is that the one perfect sacrifice is that of Christ on the cross—His death (and with it His blood) which perfectly unites God and man in the New Covenant.

4. The covenant had terms. The terms were contained in the book of the Covenant. Although there is some discussion about its specific contents it patently comprises the material from chapters 20 through 23. A covenant must have terms! The Ten Words and the ordinances are the terms to which Israel pledged herself.

The New Testament has terms too. In the narrower sense it is that God provides redemption in the cross and resurrection of Christ and that man responds by faith and obedience. In the larger sense the New Testament is the terms of the New Covenant. The Latin *testamentum* is the equivalent of *covenant* so the more proper name of the New Testament is the New Covenant.

5. As we saw in chapter 19, there were unmistakable signs of the presence of Yahweh. There must also be signs of God's presence in the making of the covenant. The elders of Israel had a vision of God. No picture is described. All that is described is that they saw a magnificent blue "under his feet" (24:10). Further, the elders "saw God, and they ate and drank" (v. 11).

It is further said that God did not raise His hand against them. *To raise the hand against* meant to kill. Man cannot see God and live! Yet in the mercy of the covenant the elders of Israel saw as much of God as men can, and came as close to God as men can, *and still lived!* Why? Because they were entering into a sacred covenant with Yahweh. He is a God of compassion, mercy and love. He seeks man. Here we have rather than wrath, grace; rather than judgment, acceptance; rather than thunder and lightning, a sacred meal.

In the New Testament this is called peace and reconciliation. It is the perfection of the Old Testament concept of *shalom.* In the New Testament it is the Spirit witnessing with our spirits that we are the sons of God (or of the covenant) that gives Christians the sense of the divine Presence.

9

Get in Touch, Stay in Touch

Exodus 24:12—27:21

God as a God of love and grace redeems Israel from the iron furnace. God as a God of holiness and justice binds His redeemed people to the highest moral mandates as covenantal terms. Now the God of glory and beauty establishes a system of worship for the covenant people.

This is a necessary sequence. No worship is acceptable if there is "sin in the camp." Therefore the Ten Words must precede the Tabernacle and its system of worship. But as we have seen, morality is based on redemption and there can be no Ten Words until there is redemption from Egypt.

The prophets say much the same thing. Israel's whole worship system with its sacrifices and its holy days means nothing if there is gross injustice and sin in Israel. The worth of worship is based on the moral integrity of the worshipers. But behind both worship and morality is redemption. This is the meaning of our Lord's statement: "Go and learn what this means: 'I desire mercy [salvation], not sacrifice [your sacrificial system].' For I have not come to call the righteous [i.e., those preoccupied with morality], but sinners [i.e., those needing salvation]" (Matt. 9:13).

Redeemed man is called to morality; moral man is called to worship. The redeemed man shows his repentance in the quality of his moral life; he shows his gratitude in his worship.

The construction of the Tabernacle (or tent) of the testimony (to the covenant) was the worship system enjoined by the Lord upon Israel. It was part of the covenant. It showed that as redemption must be followed by morality, morality must be followed by worship.

Calvin said that there is no true knowledge of God without the worship of God. Philosophy of religion, which endlessly discusses such things as proofs for God's existence, immortality, ethics and value theory and never gets to worship is far from biblical religion. The philosopher or theologian who wants to reduce Christianity to morality or social action is also far from biblical religion. *God is to be served!* To serve God means to trust Him, to obey Him *and to worship Him.* We have not come full round if we have not come to worship.

God Wills to Dwell Within Israel—Exodus 24:15—25:9

God called Moses up into the mountain to receive another great chunk of revelation (24:15-18). He remained there for forty days and received the great revelation about the Tabernacle.

One of the names of God is The Exalted One or The Uplifted One. His beauty, His glory, His transcendence and His majesty are represented spatially in their magnitude and greatness. That He should be Companion, Friend and fellow Pilgrim seems impossible. Yet this section reveals that this is exactly what He wills to be.

God told Moses to make Him a sanctuary that He might dwell in the midst of Israel (25:8). The God who redeemed Israel from the Destroyer and then from the army of Pharaoh wished to take up residence within Israel. We emphasize *within* for the Tabernacle was to be in the center of the camp.

God chooses to dwell in a holy building called a temple. A temple cannot be picked up and moved around. So a portable temple in the form of a tent must be constructed. Hence we have the Tabernacle. *Tabernacle* is derived from the Latin word for tent, *tabernaculum. Tent* is the better translation of the Hebrew word *ohel.* In context it means a sacred tent. As the tent of testimony, it means the tent that contains the book of the Covenant recording the covenant made at Mount Sinai.

The Tabernacle[1] is to be made according to the divine plan (25:9). God is to be worshiped as He prescribes, not as man thinks.

This is also in keeping with the structure of divine revelation. Biblical religion is a divine gift of grace through revelation, not an achievement of man's questing spirit. The Tabernacle is God's gracious gift—given with instructions concerning how God wishes man to worship Him.

It is always God's will to dwell in a temple. The greatest of all temples is the body of Christ. "The Word became flesh and lived for a while [tented] among us" (see John 1:14). The body of the believer is a temple of the Holy Spirit. The church also is a temple of the living Spirit. Finally, the eternal Temple of God is the New Jerusalem.

The Ark as the Symbol of the Presence of God—Exodus 25:10-16

The description of the Tabernacle begins with its most important piece (Exod. 25:10-16). We call the items in the Tabernacle *furniture* for lack of a better name. Of course they were not furniture in the modern sense of the word but special pieces that functioned in the worship of Yahweh.

The ark was 27 inches wide by 45 inches long by 27 inches deep. It was a very expensive piece of furniture for it was overlaid with gold. The word *ark* means a chest or a box and is a different word from Noah's ark and from the ark in which Jochebed put Moses.

More than any other piece of furniture it stood for the presence of God in the midst of Israel. It led the Israelites in their pilgrimage to Palestine and it led the armies of Israel in war. Inside were the Ten Commandments. It was customary in those days to have covenants made "before the gods" in some sort of container. So Israel's covenant with God was in the ark in the presence of God as a continuous witness of the terms. Also in the ark were the oracles of God given from time to time.

God was not in the box. The presence of God was symbolized by the Shekinah Glory. The ark thus represented God as His surrogate but it did not contain God.

To the Christian the ark speaks of Christ who also was the surrogate of the presence of God. In Him the Shekinah Glory (God's manifested glory) truly dwelled (see John 1:14). As Lord He also is the leader of the people of God. He goes before us in our daily life. And He is the seal and terms of the covenant of grace.

meal. As a meal it stands for the sacred meal that united Israel and Yahweh in the Sinaitic covenant.

3. As a meal offering it represents the continuous sacrifice of Israel before Yahweh.

4. Leviticus 24:5-8 suggests that the twelve loaves represent the twelve tribes of Israel and their continued presence before Yahweh.

The Lampstand—the Lord Is the Light of My Life—Exodus 25:31-40

A lampstand was a means of permanently resting a lamp high enough off the floor so that it would shed its light over a wide area. Archeologists have unearthed all sorts of lampstands from very simple to very elaborate constructions.

Again we have a hint of the nature of the lampstand from a very graphic relief on the Arch of Titus mentioned previously. This lampstand is very heavy in its design and must have been heavy to carry, as implied by the number of men carrying it on the relief of the arch. Other pictures of it are found on coins and synagogue walls. The "Menorah" as it is called is one of the great symbols of Judaism.

Its obvious service was to cast light in the darkened holy place. Some interpreters think this was its only function. In view of the rich symbolism of the Tabernacle, it would be odd for an object to be mentioned without a deeper meaning.

Light is so frequently associated with God in the Old Testament that that possible symbolism cannot be overlooked. Nor can we ignore the many places where it is said that God grants light or that men walk in His light.

The New Testament carries through both motifs (that God is light and that He gives the light of life to human kind). It adds to this the great Christological motif: Christ is the Light of the world (see John 1:9; 8:12; 9:5; 12:46).

The lamp and the lampstand are the surety that God will always be the Light of Israel. The number seven expresses fullness and this in turn affirms the degree to which God shall be the Light of Israel. According to the New Testament, light is truth! To walk in truth is to walk in light. How shall God be truth to Israel? The institutionalized answer to this question is the order of the prophet. The prophets are uniquely the men of the Word of God. It is the Word of Yahweh which they shall have revealed to them, which in turn they shall preach and write, that will be the light of Yahweh to Israel!

Curtains Form the Shrine of God's Holy Things—Exodus 26:1-14

The roof or actual tent is formed by ten curtains. Obviously the function of all the curtains (vv. 7-14) was to shut out the weather and the sunlight, for the light of the holiest of holies was the Shekinah Glory and the lampstand provided light for the holy place.

Nothing anywhere suggests the symbolism of the curtains. The one clue is that sacred things are always protected things. *Profane* means "before the temple" and hence outside its sacred protection. The holiness of what is on the inside is thus protected by proper covering.

The Boards—Fabric of the Tent, Symbol of the People of God—Exodus 26:15-30

The Tabernacle had to be portable and had to exclude light. Also in some ways it anticipated the Temple. The boards gave the Tabernacle rigidity, portability and the exclusion of light. The Israelites had wagons to carry the heavy stuff of the Tabernacle (see Gen. 45:19,21,27; Num. 7:7,8). Pictures of wagons from Egyptian pictures are generally two-wheeled whereas those from Mesopotamia are four-wheeled.

The New Testament uses many images for the church. One of them is that of a temple (see Eph. 2:19-22; 1 Pet. 2:4,5). The New Testament says that the real temple of God is not a building but the people of God, the redeemed community in Christ. Christ is the foundation of this temple; the Holy Spirit is the workman who makes the temple and who is its inner cohesion; and Christians are "living stones" built into the temple. Also closely connected here is the idea that the church is the new exodus people of God.

It sounds odd to call Christians "living boards" but that is what it amounts to if one follows the idea of the temple as the people of God in the New Testament back to the Temple of Solomon and then back to its prototype, the Tabernacle.

Veils or Curtains, Symbols of the Principles Of Access to God—Exodus 26:31-37

The Tabernacle was divided into the holy place and the holy of holies. This involved two curtains. The first before the holy place shut out light from the horizontal direction and the second divided the holy place from the most holy place (Exod. 26:31-37).

The New Testament sees real significance in the veils, especially in the second veil. That it carried an enormous weight of symbolism is witnessed by the fact that it was split (i.e., destroyed in its role or function as a divider) at the time of the death of Christ (see Matt. 27:51).

This is further discussed by the author of Hebrews

(9:6-12). He makes the strong statement that the Holy Spirit is teaching a lesson by this veil (9:8). While this veil stood, free access to God was not possible; when it was split and Jesus went through it, it meant that the believer now has access to God immediately in His Name (9:12): "Therefore, brothers, since we have confidence to enter the Most Holy Place by the blood of Jesus, by a new and living way opened for us through the curtain, that is, his body . . . let us draw near . . . " (10:19-22).

One of the mistakes people make is thinking that access to God is based *completely on inner disposition.* If a person feels deeply and sincerely about God, that is *all* that matters. Not so! There was a veil that excluded men who thought that deeply and sincerely. There must also be a principle of access. So we are told in Hebrews. It is the atoning and reconciling death of Christ that is the objective, "in God" basis of our access to God. This is not to underplay the significance of human trust, sincerity and desire to experience God. In Scripture this is always a two-way street. There is also God's prescription for access. Some people want to eliminate God's prescriptions and base access to God purely on internal response to God. One of the great theological lessons of the Tabernacle is to show us that that is not enough. The veil must be split in two! Then we may enter boldly and freely! The throne of grace is now open access to all believers (see Heb. 4:14-16).

The Altar, the Perpetual Mender of The Covenant—Exodus 27:1-8

The Tabernacle was through and through, line by line, word by word, a structure of the covenant. It functioned for two purposes: (1) it was the means whereby Yahweh was worshiped in Israel; and (2) it was the means whereby the Israelites were kept in covenantal relationship despite their misdeeds.

Accordingly the first article of furniture in the courtyard and at the gate or "door" was the bronze altar (Exod. 27:1-8). Here is where the animals of sacrifice were slain and burned. All the blood carried into the most holy place originated here. The sacrifices are described in detail in Leviticus 1—8.

An ancient altar was a natural outcropping of rock or a pile or mound of dirt or a pile of stones. Israel's altar had to be portable so it was made of metal. In that old world, altars and sacrifices and religion were all related. We should not wonder. God must teach us the higher by lessons in the lower; God must reach us at the level in which we can understand Him. As odd as altars and sacrifices are to us today, they were part of the education of the race necessary to understand the cross.

A sacrifice always meant the death of an animal *before* God. Animals might be killed for food or put to death because they were suffering or dangerous. By killing an animal before the altar its sacrificial character was delimited or marked out. It was not the nicest object lesson! Even Calvin with his strong theological stomach was repelled by the vision of burning, smelling and smoking animal carcasses! However, the concept of sacrifice is one of the most powerful means of conveying the significance of the death of Christ. The book of Hebrews makes a direct connection between the animal sacrifices of the Old Testament and the death of Jesus Christ (see Heb. 13:10-15). He even says of Christians: "We have an altar" (v. 10).

When Paul said, "For I resolved to know nothing while

I was with you except Jesus Christ and him crucified" (1 Cor. 2:2) we immediately get the picture of the cross at the door or gate of the temple of God as the first great truth sinners must confront as they seek salvation from God.

The Wall of Curtains and the Principles of Inclusion and Exclusion—Exodus 27:9-21

All temples of the old world manifested the two principles of inclusion and exclusion. The principle of inclusion meant that within these walls was something holy. It was holy in that it had to do with the gods. The sanctity of the gods was proclaimed and protected by their being hidden behind walls. The principle of exclusion meant that access to the gods was not any man's prerogative. Only certified people (priests) by certified methods (rituals, sacrifices and so on) could enter the precinct of the sacred.

The Tabernacle and the Temple were no exception to the principles of inclusion and exclusion (Exod. 27:9-21). The linen walls although fragile as walls proclaimed the same message as though they had been made of brick or heavy stones. The people of Israel were kept out of the holy places! Sinners were not permitted to tread the sacred court without proper sacrifice! The people were excluded because the walls included the holy things—but more than that, God Himself as the Shekinah Glory. It was because of what the Tabernacle included that there was also an exclusion.

As we learned from the veils all of this has a certain symbolism. As covenantal people, the Israelites were permitted in the territory about the Tabernacle; the ordinary priests could enter the holy place as well as the Tabernacle area; but only the high priest could enter the most holy place and that once a year and only with blood. One finds all this discussed in Hebrews 9 and 10 so we are not forcing the issue to mention it here. And the truth about the veils pertains generally to the wall of curtains.

God is holy, therefore there must forever be a distinction between God and man, God and the creation, the sacred and the profane, the holy and the secular. If God is not the transcendent God of holiness, majesty and glory He is not worthy of our love nor our fear, nor is He a fit object for our worship.

The great message of the gospel is that God has reconciled the world to Himself (see 2 Cor. 5:16-21). There is free access to God in view of the great act of reconciliation wrought in Christ at the cross (v. 21). The walls are up as the perpetual sign of God's holiness; but the door and the veils are open as the perpetual sign of God's forgiveness to believing man in Jesus Christ.

Note

1. We do not know exactly how the Tabernacle was constructed. A few scholars think it was like our modern pitched tent but most reconstructions presume a boxlike rectangular structure. One such portable tent has been reconstructed by archeologists and it has the latter shape. We have some idea of several articles of furniture within it from the relief on the Arch of Titus. But it is difficult to go from a verbal description to a pictorial representation.

place, and then once a year and only with blood. Once a [illegible] all this because of [illegible] Hebrews 9 and 10 so we are not left [illegible] the issue [illegible] where, and [illegible] about the [illegible] generally to the wall of partitions.

God is holy; therefore there must forever be a distinction between God and man [illegible] the sacred and the profane, the holy and the secular. If God is not the transcendent God of holiness, majesty and glory He is not worthy of our love and our fear, nor [illegible] the object of our worship.

The great message of the gospel is that God has reconciled the world to Himself (see 2 Cor. 5:18,19). There is free access to God in view of the great act of atonement wrought in Christ at the cross (v. 21). The walls are up as a perpetual sign of God's holiness, but the door and the [illegible] as a perpetual sign of God's forgiveness to [illegible] in Jesus Christ.

10

Giving God What He Deserves

Exodus 28:1—31:18

The Beautiful Garments of the Priests—Exodus 28:1-43

The text now introduces us to the fact that the Tabernacle would be served by a priesthood. They were to be dressed in keeping with the beauty of the entire Tabernacle. Some of the outstanding features of this chapter are:

1. The priests were summoned or appointed. They did not volunteer. This is in keeping with the book of Hebrews which indicates that priests serve by divine appointment (see Heb. 5:4).

2. The garments were for "dignity and honor" (Exod. 28:2). They adorned the Tabernacle like the other precious materials. They served also as a uniform to identify the priests for their special function in Israel. The priests were thus marked men and could be known for their ministry in the service of God.

3. The Tabernacle was a holy place. The beauty of the garments expressed this holiness. Further, the plate of gold which the high priest wore had written on it: "HOLY TO THE LORD" (v. 36). This also emphasized the holiness of the Tabernacle.

4. The role of a priest was to represent men before

God. The priests of Israel were to represent all of Israel. To express this the priest had two stones with the names of the twelve tribes written on them set on the shoulder piece of the ephod or "vestment."

In addition there was the beautiful and elaborate "breastpiece of decision" (v. 29). Twelve precious stones were arranged to represent the twelve tribes of Israel: "Whenever Aaron enters the Holy Place, he will bear the names of the sons of Israel over his heart on the breastpiece of decision as a continuing memorial before the LORD" (v. 29).

5. The priesthood was regarded with tremendous seriousness because it was a priesthood before God. If the priest did things improperly the priest would die. Leviticus 10 records the death of Nadab and Abihu who trespassed the law of the Tabernacle. It was no light thing to be in the presence of the living God and the Shekinah Glory (see Exod. 28:35,38,43).

6. The priesthood also carried with it a means of knowing the will of God. This was in the Urim and Thummim. The two Hebrew words are so difficult that most translations simply transliterate the words. There is some evidence for the translation of "Light and Truth." Once there was an established order of the prophet the function of the Urim and Thummim ceased.

The intent of the Urim and Thummim is clear: *the covenant people must know the will of Yahweh to properly keep within the covenant.* How the two stones worked we do not know but certain things stand out: (a) It appears that only the head of Israel could make use of the function of the two stones; (b) They could be consulted only about matters impossible for man to know by ordinary human means; (c) A question had to be posed so it could be answered yes or no; (d) Not more than one question could be posed at a time; (e) It was an answer given by lot.

The theory that one of the stones glowed for a yes and the other for a no is not generally accepted. Perhaps in some way one stone could be picked over the other and one was the "yes" stone and the other the "no" stone.

The view that has the most hearing is that the two stones were thrown like dice. Each had a "yes" and "no" side. The answer would be yes only if both dice came up yes. Any other combination (no-no, no-yes, yes-no) was a no. It was like matching two coins where only a two-heads combination would win. Hence it would be a one-to-four possibility for a yes and hence a yes would suggest divine providence.

The theological implications of the chapter are obvious: (a) God is a God of dignity and honor and is to be worshiped not only in a beautiful movable temple but by beautifully dressed priests; (b) God is a God of unimpeachable holiness and if His place of worship is desecrated, men die; (c) a priesthood is representative and hence vicarious; and (d) prayer and spiritual commerce move in both directions—from the priests to God and from the Urim and Thummim to the priests back to the Israelites. All of this has its New Testament parallels.

The Ordination or Consecration of the Priesthood—Exodus 29:1-37

The theme of chapter 29 is stated in verse 9: "In this way you shall ordain Aaron and his sons." The process of ordination comprised four steps: (a) washing (v. 4); (b) anointing with oil (v. 7); (c) sacrifices (vv. 10 ff.); and (d) anointing with blood (vv. 19-21).

The washing was a ceremonial purification and speaks

to the truth that holiness is moral purity on behalf of man. Those who serve God must be clean vessels.

The anointing with oil coincides with the whole charismatic notion of the service of God in the Old Testament. All human talents need that special touch of the Holy Spirit. Israel did not crown her kings but anointed them to be kings. If true to their calling they were charismatic kings. The Messiah was literally the "Anointed One," for the Messiah must be filled with the Spirit to be a charismatic king as well as a royal and legal king.

The sacrifices were three in number: the sin offering (29:10-14) which was a sacrifice especially of expiation; the ram (29:15-18) which was a sweet-savour sacrifice ("pleasing aroma," v. 18) which speaks of sacrifice as a gift given to God; and the peace offering (29:19-34) which was a sacrifice of reconciliation and the "ram for the ordination." Included in this was the wave offering (29:22-26) which means that they who served the altar lived from the altar.

The general idea here is discussed in Hebrews 9:25,26. These priests needed these sacrifices for their own forgiveness, perfecting and sanctification before God. Christ is without spot and is in need of no such sacrifices. The sacrifices speak of many things. They speak of the holiness of God, for only purified priests could come into His presence. They speak of the sin of man, for man must be cleansed and made acceptable before he can serve God. They speak of their own power even though limited to fit man for the service of God. They speak futuristically of the Lamb of God who would put an end to this entire ritual for it was all shadow, type and temporary.

Finally the altar was sanctified (29:36,37). That which bore the bodies of the sacrificial animals and served the purposes of the priests must itself be made holy to be able to function.

How different is the servant of God in the New Testament church! World redemption has been accomplished in Christ's sacrifice on the cross. There is no more need of an earthly tabernacle, an earthly priesthood and animal sacrifices. Although the church as a whole is a kingdom of priests, the New Testament never uses the word *priest (hierus)* to characterize the servants in the church. Rather, they are ministers of the Word of God or of reconciliation. Once the great act of atonement had been accomplished, that was the only kind of service of God possible.

Consecration Is a Daily Affair—Exodus 29:38-46

A new development different from the ordination and consecration of the priests begins at verse 38 of chapter 29. In this section Israel's priests are told to sacrifice a lamb ("a year old") every morning and every evening that they serve in the Tabernacle. This has been called *the continual burnt offering* or *the daily burnt offering.* It included a drink offering or a libation. Libation is a form of sacrifice in that something is poured out on the ground or on the altar so that it cannot be retrieved and drunk.

The purpose of the daily burnt offering was to remind the priesthood and Israel that the covenant was maintained only through sacrifice. Man is such a sinner and God is so holy that a covenantal arrangement is in need of constant renewal and recleansing. There is a marked contrast between that twice daily sacrifice and the one great yearly sacrifice of the Day of Atonement described in Leviticus 16. Each speaks to a point. One speaks of the necessity for a daily sacrifice that continuously renews the covenant.

The other speaks of the necessity for one great big "clean-up" sacrifice every year to take care of all that has been neglected or overlooked.

The Christian counterpart of the daily burnt offering is stated by Paul in Romans 12:1,2. "I urge you, brothers in view of God's mercy, to offer your bodies as living sacrifices, holy and pleasing to God—which is your spiritual worship. Do not conform any longer to the pattern of this world, but be transformed by the renewing of your mind. Then you will be able to test and approve what God's will is—his good, pleasing and perfect will."

The chapter closes with a magnificent summary statement. God would dwell among His people in the Tabernacle and with the priests and their sacrifices. God would continue His revelation in Israel. And Israel would know that He is her God. Again we are back to Exodus 3. How would Israel know that the Lord is her God? By all the things that He would do. And what had He done? He had brought His people out of Egypt and He had preserved them in the wilderness from starvation, thirst and enemies; He had given them the law and He had given them the covenant; He had given them the Tabernacle and He had given them the priesthood. From all this, Israel now knew!

Then comes the magnificent signature: "I am the LORD their God" (Exod. 29:46). It was Calvin who said that that which characterizes the Scripture so that we might know it is the divine Word, is its *majesty*. Here is one of the marks of its majesty: the majestic signature of God. All is true because God affirms Himself. How far from a purely rational view of God! How far from the thin gruel of "comparative religions"! How this transcends religion thought of as "a value-producing process"! Who would ever worship a process or sacrifice to an all-pervasive yet indefinite world Spirit?

What a signature: "I am the LORD their God!" It brings back again Exodus 15:11, "Who among the gods is like you, O LORD? Who is like you—majestic in holiness, awesome in glory, working wonders?"

The Altar of Incense in the Worship of Yahweh—Exodus 30:1-10

The use of incense in the worship of the gods is a universal phenomenon in the temples of the ancient world kingdoms down through the Greeks and the Romans. Yet no clear "theology of incense" emerges from a historical study of incense. Some writers think that incense was believed to drive out demons and others that it was held that just as a king's palace should smell nice so should God's Temple.

There was an altar of incense in the holy place for the worship of God. The text does not tell us how it was used but it does indicate three things: (a) that incense was to be burned only by official persons; (b) that no foreign or undesignated materials were to be burned; and (c) that atonement for the altar had to be made once a year with blood. The death of Nadab and Abihu seems to be connected with their use of wrong substances in worship, perhaps by their being drunk (see Lev. 10:8-11).

Incense was used in tribute to a great king and perhaps this explains the presence of incense in the Tabernacle. God is the king of the earth and incense is the sweet-smelling material that heralds the presence of the King. Perhaps because the incense smoke rises upwards it becomes the symbol of prayer. In Luke 1:10 we are told that the people were praying at the hour of incense (see also Ps. 141:2, Rev. 5:8; 8:3,4).

The Census and the True Believer—Exodus 30:11-16

Taking a census goes back in human history as far as there are chronicles about what kings did. Kings took censuses either for taxing purposes or for military purposes or both. The census reported in this passage was a religious census. The covenant had been ratified and now the covenant members were to be ascertained through counting and the payment of half a shekel.

There seemed to be some fear of a census in Israel. No reason can be pinned down with certainty but Scripture suggests that the exact knowledge of the number of a people was God's prerogative. Man was not to infringe on this knowledge.

In this instance, however, a count was necessary. Again the text (30:11-16) does not say clearly why. The most likely reason has been suggested above: *it was the manner in which the covenant was made personal, for a man was not only counted but he paid his half shekel.* Statements like "pay the LORD a ransom for his life . . . then no plague will come on them" (v. 12), and "making atonement" (v. 16) strongly imply that far more than counting noses was involved. It was each Israelite, by being willing to be counted and paying his half shekel, owning up to the covenant and its terms.

Biblical faith is always personal. Promises must always be validated by faith. The call of revelation is a call to decision. Covenantal terms summon man to obedience. The gospel always goes out as good news and a summons to decision—to be counted.

The Basin Which Cleanses—Exodus 30:17-21

The basin is a place for washing. Again the spiritual is taught through the material. Physical cleansing conveys a message about spiritual cleansing. The priests who busied themselves with holy things should themselves be holy people (vv. 17-21).

There are many passages of Scripture in both the Old and the New Testaments that speak of washing and of water. It is one of the most persistent biblical themes. It is either God's power to cleanse man; or God's demand that His servants be morally clean people.

The Sacred Anointing Oil—Exodus 30:22-38

Three things were used in the Tabernacle to sanctify men and things: blood, water and oil. This section gives directions for the sacred anointing oil. The sacred oil could not be duplicated for general purposes; nor could it be put on an ordinary person; nor could it be put on a non-Israelite; nor could it be made otherwise than according to specifications.

The point made here as throughout this section is that all things were made by divine plan and therefore could not be altered. It is God who tells man how He wills to be worshiped. Therefore any variation of this worship is contrary to the divine will. Again this concept goes counter to the idea that religion is man's quest for God and that sincerity alone is adequate in religion.

The Gift of the Spirit for Works of Art—Exodus 31:1-11

Everything in the Tabernacle was a work of art for which God especially endowed men. It involved remarkable ability to sew the curtains and garments, it required skill to shape the articles of furniture and it required an artist's hand to make the engravings. This work could not be farmed out to Egyptian craftsmen. Israel was in a wilderness.

The problem was solved by the gifts of the Holy Spirit. The Spirit of God (*Elohim*) would fill Bezalel and Oholiab "with skill, ability and knowledge in all kinds of crafts—to make artistic designs for work in gold, silver and bronze, to cut and set stones, to work in wood, and to engage in all kinds of craftsmanship" (31:3-5).

1. The Holy Spirit was present in Israel! His presence had already been implied in 28:3. But had He not been with Israel all the time? Was not Moses a charismatic leader as well as a wise, natural leader? The Spirit of God is always with God's people. That is why both Israel and the church survive stupidity and heresy within themselves and why both survive the wicked sword of persecution and the drugging effect of the temptations of the world.

2. The Holy Spirit is the Spirit of art and beauty. How seldom that note has been sounded in Christian theology. Too much of our thinking of the Spirit has been in terms of power and endowment. God as a God of glory is thereby a God of beauty. If God willed a beautiful Tabernacle there must be something beautiful about God, some divine concern for beauty. If that is true of God, it is also true of the Spirit of God.

3. It is a Jewish tradition that God never gives a gift from His Spirit to a man unless the man already has some natural endowment or has educated himself in that skill. This seems to be the point made here. Bezalel and Oholiab were artists in their own right. They received an additional empowering of the Spirit to do the specific tasks for the Tabernacle.

Something similar occurs in Acts 6:3 where the early church chose men on the grounds that they were full of wisdom as well as of the Holy Spirit. God wants all that we can give Him in natural endowments and educated abilities; in turn He wants to give us that something extra that can come only from His Holy Spirit.

The Sabbath Applies to the Construction of The Tabernacle—Exodus 31:12-17

The Sabbath had been mentioned in 16:22-30 and with the Ten Commandments (20:8-11). In the latter reference as here (vv. 12-17), the basis for the Sabbath is the week of creation. Man is to imitate in his life the pattern of God in creation. Six days of work is to be followed by the seventh day of rest.

In this connection *work* was understood primarily as heavy manual work or any kind of occupational labor. After the artists were commissioned to build the Tabernacle (as mentioned in the preceding section) the question might have arisen whether the Sabbath pertained to the sacred work of building the Tabernacle. The answer was that it did. Bezalel, Oholiab and their crews were to observe the Sabbath even though working on the sacred Tabernacle.

Perhaps the message here is that people who do God's work in a special way are not exempt from the moral and spiritual considerations that God binds on all men. Anybody in gospel work or church work does at times feel that he or she is exempt from the laws of the state, if not moral and spiritual principles. There can well be an extreme case where such a feeling may be justified, but it had better be an extreme case! God is best served by those who best keep His Word, not by those who forever find themselves exemptions to it.

11

In the Gap for Others

Exodus 31:18—32:35

Israel Is Out of Egypt but Egypt Isn't Out of Israel—Exodus 31:18—32:35

In 31:18 we have a summary statement: God concluded His revelation to Moses on Mount Sinai, giving him the tables of stone containing the Ten Words "inscribed by the finger of God."

In the meantime something else was going on in the camp. Chapter 32 is the Romans 7 of the book of Exodus. It tells of a terrible incongruity—like a murder in a cathedral during a high mass or a rape at a wedding feast or goofing clowns at a funeral. Something occurs that is entirely out of place.

In the midst of a high and holy revelation, in the midst of the manifestation of the glory of God, a terrible incident of idolatry occurred, accompanied by gross immoral behavior.

Paul refers to is: "Do not be idolaters, as some of them were; as it is written: 'The people sat down to eat and drink and got up to indulge in pagan revelry'" (1 Cor. 10:7).

The psalmist speaks of it: "At Horeb they made a calf and worshiped an idol cast from metal. They exchanged their glory for an image of a bull, which eats grass. They forgot the God who had saved them, who had done great things in Egypt, miracles in the land of Ham and awesome deeds by the Red Sea. So he said he would destroy them—had not Moses, his chosen one, stood in the breach before him to keep his wrath from destroying them" (Ps. 106:19-23).

Ezekiel also mentions it: "And I said to them, 'Each of you get rid of the vile images you have set your eyes on, and do not defile yourselves with the idols of Egypt. I am the LORD your God. But they rebelled against me and would not listen to me; they did not get rid of the vile images they had set their eyes on, nor did they forsake the idols of Egypt" (20:7,8).

It is shocking. How could such depravity break out in the midst of such holiness? How could gratitude for redemption from the slavery of Egypt so soon give way to idolatrous worship?

But is it so strange? Was there not the case of infamous lying by Ananias and Sapphira in the infant Christian church—so near Calvary and the Resurrection? Do we not find terrible sexual sins among the Corinthians who were not lacking in spiritual gifts? Evangelists of the nineteenth century knew that men who were at the mourners' bench Sunday night were to be found drunk in the saloon on Monday night. Thousands of young people who have a great mountaintop experience in some Christian camp in the summertime are found back in their old fleshly patterns in the winter season. Our Lord spoke of those who would spring up with a healthy green at the hearing of the gospel but who would wither away when the hot sun of persecution arose (see Matt. 13:5,6,20,21).

None of us is far from Egypt! The food, the idols, and the dances of Egypt lurk in the hinterland of our consciousness. What a little event brings it into the foreground of our life! Israel marched out of Egypt, but Egypt did not march out of Israel!

This chapter suggests that the Israelites were spiritually immature. Perhaps we expect too much. It is only a few months since they escaped from their days of slavery. They displayed this immaturity in their frequent grumbling. It is but a step or two from grumbling to idolatry.

Asked if Christians do much better, we are hesitant to answer quickly. Christians too are but flesh! Salvation is not glorification. Christians too may march out of Egypt without Egypt marching out of them. We are all pilgrims—some strong, some weak, but all pilgrims. Even the famous saints of the church would seem less saintly if we had a careful documentation of their inner life. This is why God is infinitely patient with His children and why the whole creation groans as it awaits that final day of deliver ance from all of Egypt's influences.

This chapter also reveals how a decline from faith in God leads to a decline in morality. Once Israel abandoned its faith in Yahweh and Moses turning to idolatry, she also turned to immorality. In the expression "got up to indulge in revelry" (Exod. 32:6) there is the suggestion of immoral behavior. In verse 25 the expression "the people were running wild" means that they had given up all moral restraints.

This is the great theme of Romans 1. When man departs from a knowledge of the true God into idolatry he cannot stop there. He moves on into serious moral defections from divine righteousness. And for this reason the wrath of God is revealed from heaven. Chapter 32 shows again from the biblical perspective the folly of separating morality from true religion.

This chapter further reveals the power of idolatry. We are truly unreflective if we think idolatry is the temptation only of primitives. The visible is always more powerful to the imagination than the invisible. The image stirs the emotions more readily than the concept. That which we can approach with our bodies seems more accessible to us than that which we can approach with our souls. How easy it was for the Israelites to look at the golden calf and say: "These are your gods, O Israel, who brought you up out of Egypt" (v. 8).

John wrote: "Dear children, keep yourselves from idols" (1 John 5:21). Certainly John is not speaking of Christians worshiping little stone gods! He means that this world is itself one immense idol. As such it has many powers of fascination. It has many faces of bewitchment. As an immense idol the world at hand is more powerful to the imagination and emotions than is the eternal invisible God. Therefore even Christians must take special pains not to fall into the gravitational field of the idolatry of this world.

And what are we to think of Aaron? The Jewish commentators are very defensive about Aaron and wish to free him from all blame, or as much blame as possible. It seems psychologically impossible for them to think that the head of the priesthood could have been guilty of such actions as described in chapter 32. When we read their efforts to free Aaron of all guilt in the matter of the calf and the events surrounding it, we sense that the arguments are too forced. They protest too much. Aaron is not a supersanctified person. Even Moses, because of his own failures, was not permitted to enter the Promised Land!

Let us not be too severe on the Jewish commentators. Do not Christians constantly underrate the "old self" of Romans 6? Do we not at times claim more for Christian experience than we actually deliver? Do not we Protestants who have nothing to do with Roman Catholic saints have our own ways of canonizing our heroes? We must never charm ourselves into thinking that even the most saintly person is free from some outrageous sin. Again, salvation is not glorification even though at times we force it to seem that way. Sanctification is not perfection even though we pretend that it is. No, we are all Aarons, and Aaron is just like us!

The most encouraging aspect of this chapter is the intercessory work of Moses. Here is an amazing spiritual fact. Men may intercede with God for their fellow men and succeed!

Alfred North Whitehead, a famous philosopher of the recent past, rejected the God of the Old Testament because He was a God of stern moralism. His knowledge of the Old Testament must have been very superficial. Already in Exodus, God has said that He will hear the cry of the man shivering from cold because a ruthless lender has kept his garment from him. The text reads: "When he cries out to me, I will hear, for I am compassionate" (Rom. 22:27). Here the compassionate God is not God of stern, unbending moralism. Again in this account of Moses' intercession with God, here is no God of stern, unbending moralism but a compassionate God.

This fact becomes more evident when the Scripture says that God "relented and did not bring on his people the disaster he had threatened" (Exod. 32:14). This is called an *anthropopathism.* It means to speak of God as though

He suffered, felt, reacted like a human being. To speak of God repenting is an *anthropopathism.* It reveals that God is a God of tender feelings, and responds to our prayers, petitions and predicaments.

Moses' first intercession was based on the possibility that the news that Israel had been destroyed would certainly get back to the Egyptians and they would say, "We were right after all. The God of the Hebrews led them into the wilderness only to destroy them." Then he appealed to the covenantal promises God had made to the patriarchs (vv. 11-13).

An even stronger intercession by Moses is recorded in verses 30-34. For Israel's sake, Moses is willing to have his name blotted out of God's book. The book is either a list of the living, from which to be blotted out means to die, or else it is a list of the members of the Kingdom of God analogous to the list that ancient kings kept of their royal subjects.

Whatever the interpretation, the message of both intercessions by Moses in this chapter is clear: intercessory prayer for fellow believers does get through to God. Petitionary prayer is part of a believer's spiritual life. God has willed that prayer count, and therefore it does count. It is with good reason that some theologians have said the real test of any theology is its theology of prayer. The theology of prayer structures the whole divine-human relationship.

Why does the text speak of gods (vv. 8,23,31) when Aaron made just one idol? Jewish and Roman Catholic interpreters take the plural as the plural of majesty. Hence a plural intends a singular, just as Elohim is plural but intends just one God. Or else as some Jewish commentators understand it (in their attempt to defend Aaron) it means Yahweh and this God brought Israel out of Egypt. They interpret the idol as being more a substitute throne for that of the cherubim in the Tabernacle than an independent god. Other commentators take it as speaking of the gods of Jeroboam (see 1 Kings 14:9) of which this passage is a projection backwards. There is no ready solution to this problem.

How could Moses have ground up a golden calf? The most accepted explanation is that the calf was made of wood and then covered with gold. Hence it was the wood that he ground up. Moses ground it up to show how helpless and worthless was the god that the Israelites worshiped.

What did it mean to drink the water with the pulverized calf in it (v. 20)? Some commentators think it was a crude lie-detector test like that given to the suspected woman in Numbers 5:16-31. Perhaps closer to the truth is the thought that when he says that it was the ultimate step in repudiating the idolatry of the people: they had to drink the remains of their idol!

The most obscure and difficult part of the chapter is the part played by the Levites. They defied their leader, Aaron, and refrained from both the idolatry and the reveling. Some commentators take this to be an alternative account of the founding of the priesthood. We simply must confess that this is one of those obscure parts of Scripture the Reformers spoke of that must be understood by the clear parts.

God's Presence Must Be Renegotiated—Exodus 33:1-6

God's reaction to the idolatry and reveling of Israel was to tell Moses that He would no longer be with Israel in her journey to Palestine (v. 3). He would send an angel before them as a surrogate (v. 2). The Israelites were to go immediately up to the land and so no longer be under God's supernatural support. Further as a sign of mourning they were to take off all their ornaments. God accused them of being stiff-necked like a very stubborn animal.

This is a very hard line. The Israelites never guessed how critical their great sin (32:31) was. The most devastating of punishments would be to continue their existence without the presence of the living God with them as Provider and Protector!

God's message got through. The people mourned. How paradoxical! While Moses was up in the mountain how enthusiastically they turned to idolatry and dancing. When they heard the solemn charge in this passage they mourned and stripped their ornaments from themselves.

This variability is "on target" with regard to spiritual life. We presume that believers are constant in their faith; experience proves otherwise. Pulsations of strength and/or weakness are every pilgrim's lot.

God's People Need God's Word—Exodus 33:7-11

On the slow journey from Egypt to Palestine, life went on for the Israelites. In their communal living certainly many problems arose beyond their powers to settle. The only recourse they knew of was God. He alone had the wisdom to resolve the problems. God's people needed God's Word.

In order for God's people to receive a word (an oracle) from God, Moses pitched a special tent. There seem to be three tents in Exodus: the sacred tent used as a very preliminary temple before the building of the Tabernacle; then the Tabernacle proper; finally, this special tent for the divine word or oracle for the difficult problems of the Israelites. Whether the distance of the tent from the camp suggested God's anger with Israel for her idolatry or whether it was to keep a distance between God's glory (33:10) and the people, the text does not say.

If a man really needed a word from the Lord he then passed his problem on to Moses and Moses consulted the Lord. The procedure is described in Exodus 33:7-11.[1] On such occasions the pillar of the cloud would descend and all the people would know that the Lord was communicating with Moses.[2] It says that the Lord talked face to face with Moses (v. 11). A commentary on this is found in Numbers 12:8: "With him (Moses) I speak face to face, clearly and not in riddles; he sees the form of the LORD." These passages reveal a directness of communication not experienced by any other prophet in the history of Israel. Moses was in no trance nor ecstatic state but the communication was as direct as possible. For this reason, Moses is the theologian of the Old Testament.

Until there was a canonical Scripture, God had to make this kind of adjustment for man. Life is too complex for human wisdom, even the wisest of men. Yet to live our lives so as to please God we need from time to time a word from God.

In the Christian church we have no such word. Perhaps the early church did under the gift of prophecy, but this was not for the total length of church history. God has given the church the New Testament. Whatever word from the Lord we need will be found in the Bible. This is a precious heritage and although it does not answer every conceivable question that can arise in the church, it is the greatest and best light we have.

Moses Needs Spiritual Renewal—Exodus 33:12-23

Perhaps the previous section on the tent where oracles were given was to explain the intimate conversation that followed (Exod. 33:12-23). Not that the conversation took place in the tent (see vv. 21,22), but the kind of conversations that Moses had in the tent were typical of his conversations with Yahweh.

The central problem harks back to the beginning of this chapter when the Lord said that He would no longer go with Israel but would send a surrogate angel in His place (v. 2). Moses didn't think that Israel could make it on those terms.

Further, reading between the lines, we get the impression that Moses was shaken up in his sense of leadership. Israel's lapse into idolatry seems to have rocked his sense of competency as a leader. Perhaps he felt as though he needed something more—a new vision of God—if he was to carry on as the leader. We have in this section a very intense conversation between Yahweh and Moses.

Moses wanted two things very much if he was to continue as leader: (a) he wanted to know the ways of God (v. 13) for he was feeling confused. How could he continue to lead this stiff-necked people without knowing how the Lord planned to manage them? (b) He wanted to be sure that God would be present. Therefore he made a very unusual request: "show me your glory" (v. 18). Moses was seeking a visible, dramatic appearance of God so that he would know that God's presence still was with him and the people.

God granted this request to see His glory but on certain terms: Moses could not see the undiminished glory of

God and live (v. 20). Moses was not to think that he had cornered God. God responded in His pure sovereign grace: "I will have mercy on whom I will have mercy, and I will have compassion on whom I will have compassion" (v. 19).

There is another fascinating aspect of this special manifestation of the glory of God. God would make all His goodness pass before Moses. Glory and goodness are synonyms in this passage. However, in some passages *tov* means beauty. Hence beauty and glory are synonyms. Again we have an aspect of God generally ignored by theologians and even more by preachers. God is a beautiful God!

Because the glory of God is so overwhelming Moses could not see it nor the fullness of it directly. God had to place him in the cleft of a rock, covering Moses with His hand so that he could see only the back of God. These expressions are anthropomorphic—God is spoken of in human terms. How else could it be? The passage does not narrate that all this took place but it evidently did. Moses was now revived and ready to carry on as the leader of Israel.

Another interesting verse is verse 16, "How will anyone know that you are pleased with me and with your people unless you go with us? What else will distinguish me and your people from all the other people on the face of the earth?" If we focus our attention upon Israel too intently all we will see is Israel lost in the sands of the Sinaitic Peninsula. But this verse expands our vision so that now the whole earth is within our perspective. Yahweh is not only the God of this little nation out on this little part of the earth, but the God of all nations! The God who elected Israel out of all nations also knows that these other nations exist. The Scriptures do concentrate on Israel. That may give the appearance that God is a typical national and cultic deity. But this verse prevents that, for the God of all the nations of the world is not a national, provincial, cultic God.

Notes

1. There is the suggestion that the tent might be abused by an overzealous Israelite who would want a word without "going through procedures." So Joshua was stationed permanently in the tent (v. 11) to prevent such an occurrence. Here and there the text suggests the great role Joshua would play in the future as well as his sterling character.

2. Perhaps the reason the cloud came down in the sight of all Israel when Moses consulted the Lord was to assure the people that the decision was not Moses' personal one but truly the word from the Lord.

12

The Compassionate God Is with Us

Exodus 34:1—40:38

The Intercession Is Successful—Exodus 34:1-9

The two main themes of chapter 34 are that the covenant is renewed and that the Lord promises to go with the Israelites. The whole chapter is a magnificent witness to Moses' power of intercession before God.

In this chapter also we have a second great revelation of the nature of God. Exodus 3:14 was highly suggestive; this chapter is wonderfully detailed. The Jewish scholars call it the "Thirteen Attributes of Yahweh."

God proclaims His name! He comes and says to Moses, "The LORD, the LORD" (v. 6). Let us spell out what the Lord says in proclaiming His name, i.e., His essence, His character, His nature: compassionate, gracious, slow to anger, abounding in love and faithfulness, maintaining love to thousands, forgiving wickedness, rebellion and sin, does not leave the guilty unpunished; punishes the children and their children to the third and fourth generation.

It should be seen that the attributes of love and grace

are balanced by attributes of righteousness and holiness. This is why many theologians define Yahweh as righteous love.

The contrast between God's love and His wrath is also very great. His love continues to thousands of generations, His wrath but to the third and fourth. The only expression that conveys the love of God more bountifully is John 3:16—"that he gave his one and only Son."

The response of Moses to God's revelation of Himself is worthy of note. In the light of God's proclamation of His name he "bowed to the ground at once, and worshiped" (v. 8). What is worship but the servant's response to the greatness of his Lord, the creature's gratitude towards his Creator, the redeemed's recognition of the magnificent bounty in the mercies of his Redeemer?

Then Moses asked God to live up to His name. If God is so merciful and compassionate, let Him "go with us" (v. 9). God had said He would not go with Israel (33:3). Now Moses appealed to God to be with Israel even though they were like a stubborn ass or a willful ox.

Of course God had already begun to respond. He promised to give Moses a second copy of the Ten Words and He pronounced His great name to Moses. The marriage between Yahweh and Israel was mended. Yahweh would go with His people. Moses' intercession had been a success.

God Will Go with Israel—Exodus 34:10-28

After the terrible breach of the covenant by Israel's unexpected lapse into idolatry, her relationship to God was gradually restored through the intercession of Moses. Now God established the covenant (vv. 10,27).

Yahweh told Moses how great this covenant arrangement would be. Yahweh would do wonders "never before done in any nation in all the world" (v. 10).

The God of redemption is a God who makes a difference. Words must be reenforced with deeds else they are mere words. Theologians and preachers who object to anything supernatural in Christianity are not talking about biblical religion. Biblical religion is more than ideas, religious thoughts or theological speculation; it is how God powerfully, realistically, and supernaturally takes part in human affairs to establish His truth, His redemption, and His Word.

Again we see that God's concern embraces the whole world (v. 10). He was not a God carted around in a box (the Ark of the Covenant) nor capsuled in the tent of meeting. He was and is the God of all mankind and of all nations. That He was with Israel resulted from an election of pure grace and sovereign love in order that one nation on the face of the earth should have the truth of God in its purity as a witness to all.

Further He would do awesome things (v. 10). These awesome things are specified in verse 11. God would drive out Israel's enemies from the land that He would give her.

God gave Moses a number of ordinances and admonitions that Israel might understand that He was renewing the covenant. He warned Israel not to let the religions of the pagan tribes in Palestine corrupt her religion. He forbade her to make a covenant with these peoples. Israel failed to follow that advice first because she was tricked into a covenant about which she did not consult the Lord (see Josh. 9:3-27), but later through her own weakness (see Ps. 106:34-39). The whole point is that it would be tragic to have escaped the idolatrous religion of Egypt only to be caught in the idolatrous religions of Palestine.

Therefore Israel was to be iconoclastic—image-breaking. Israel was to tear down pagan altars, pillars and poles. Some scholars believe the stone pillars stood for the male deities and the wooden poles for female deities—hints of the degraded nature of pagan religion at that time. The *Asherah* (Exod. 34:13) were wooden posts representing a female goddess.

The reason for this iconoclasm is that God is a God whose name is Jealous (v. 14). God is a jealous God—don't overlook the fact that Jealous is a proper name of God in the text—because He is the only God. Any other god is a usurper. How else could the one, true, holy, just, and loving God be other than a jealous God or One whose name is Jealous? Could he look indifferently at idols? at sinful representations of deity? at a grotesque pantheon of gods in some pagan temple? Is the God and Father of our Lord Jesus Christ any different?

At the conclusion of sundry ordinances which are generally a restatement, God told Moses to write down all these words for they constituted a renewal of the covenant. This Moses did (v. 28) and now the terrible breach of the covenant was mended.

The Glory of the Lord Reflected on the Face of Moses—Exodus 34:29-35

With our modern science we know how to irradiate rocks so that they will glow after they are removed from the light. Such as the experience of Moses recorded in verses 29-35. Talking with God, in the presence of the glory of God, his face had become radiant and shone even after he left the presence of God.

The interpreters are split on the precise use of the veil

by Moses. The traditional view is that Moses was without a veil when he spoke with Yahweh; he was without a veil when he spoke the Word of Yahweh to the people; then he wore a veil as he went about. The alternate interpretation is that Moses was without the veil when he spoke with Yahweh; but that when he came out from the presence of the Lord he continuously wore a veil. The record implies that Moses wore the veil so as not to frighten the Israelites.

Paul suggests that Moses wore the veil to hide the fact that the radiance on his face faded away and was renewed by again going into the presence of the Lord (see 2 Cor. 3:7-16). There seems to be a theological issue here because conservative commentators give the traditional view and nonconservatives the view that Paul makes a very curious use of the passage.

Some interpreters understand the radiant face of Moses as an anticipation of the transfiguration of Christ. Others connect it more closely with 2 Corinthians 3 as an anticipation of the glorification of believers. In either case, Paul's use of the passage indicates that there is a typological or transhistorical factor to it.

In any case the radiant face of Moses was a witness to his people that he actually talked with God and heard His Word. He did not commune with himself and due to the static electricity in the air get a radiant face. He was in an undiminished sense a prophet, a man of the Word of God.

Israel, the Unfaithful Wife, Comes Back to The Covenant—Exodus 35:1-3

It is proverbial that ceremonies for second weddings are very short. So it was with Israel. Moses simply assembled the people and announced the covenant with a minimal statement or two of what was involved.

Kindling a fire on the Sabbath is specifically mentioned as forbidden. Perhaps this had become a particular aggravation and needed a special word said about it.

The fracture was now mended. God had given a new set of tables of the law. The breach created by Israel's idolatry was now healed. The history resumes with the building of the Tabernacle, postponed by Israel's lapse. After that the Israelites would start their slow journey to Palestine.

The Fabrication of the Tabernacle According To the Divine Plan—Exodus 35:4—39:43

This passage is a recitation of how the different workmen and workwomen manufactured the different parts of the Tabernacle and sewed the garments of the priests. The significance of most of the items has been mentioned in the preceding chapters and needs no further comment here. However, there are several exceptions.

1. The principle of giving was a generous heart—a heart that had been stirred (35:5,21,22,29). The people brought so much Moses had to tell them to stop (36:5-7). It reminds us of Paul's statement "God loves a cheerful (*hilaros,* hence, hilarious) giver" (2 Cor. 9:7).

What stirred the heart of the Israelites was what the Lord had done for them from Egypt to Sinai. How else can human beings respond to such generosity of divine grace but in some tangible way showing his gratitude?

2. Women were included in this project (35:22,26,29; 38:8). The New Testament speaks of deaconnesses (see Rom. 16:1,2 and perhaps Phil. 4:2,3; 1 Tim. 3:11). No great doctrine of full respect of women can be built on such few verses but they do suggest as much.

3. This work of the Tabernacle could be done only by the gift of the holy and divine enablement (35:31-35; 36:2). This reaffirms what has been said before. The workmen were charismatic artists and artistic charismatics. The Holy Spirit used men with natural gifts; people with natural gifts submitted themselves for that "extra" that comes from the Holy Spirit.

4. When all the work was finished it was brought to Moses (39:32-43) and when Moses saw that it was done according to the divine plan he blessed the people of Israel (v. 43). Doing everything according to the pattern revealed in heaven had a serious point (see Heb. 8:1-5). Only God knows how man is to be redeemed. Only God knows which sacrifices please Him. And only God knows how He is to be worshiped. It may have been in that ancient culture that temples were to be built according to a divine plan; if so, this was literally true in Israel. Biblical religion is God's projection of His mind and His ways into our world.

What else can be said of the Christian gospel? It is not man's plan. The gospel is like the Tabernacle whose outlines were given in heaven that men on earth might copy the divine mind.

The Grand Conclusion: the Glory of God in The Midst of Israel—Exodus 40:1-38

All the articles of the Tabernacle were completed (39:43). God now told Moses to set up the Tabernacle (40:1). This was nine months after the arrival at Mount Sinai and one year and fourteen days after the Exodus from Egypt. Moses set up the Tabernacle and consecrated the priests. "So Moses finished the work" (40:33).

Moses and his helpers could make all the furnishings

and clothings. Moses could consecrate the priests. There was one thing that no man including Moses could do and that was to command the presence of God: to summon the Shekinah Glory into the holy of holies!

Now God was ready to accomplish that. Israel had been redeemed from Egypt. Israel had been given the Ten Commandments. Israel had entered into covenant with God. The Tabernacle had been built and assembled. The priests had been consecrated. Then—and only then—all was in order for the Lord to take up His residence in the Tabernacle which was in the center of the camp of Israel.

The glory of God descended and filled the Tabernacle.

The Tabernacle was no temporary dwelling of God. God would go with the people of Israel throughout all their journeys (vv. 36,38). By day, the glory of God was a cloud; by night it was a pillar of fire. In worship it was the Shekinah Glory between the cherubim in the holy of holies.

The book of Exodus ends and what an ending it is!

Bibliography

Basic Resource Books

The following were continuously consulted for historical and geographical materials and all other matters mentioned in the text:

Orr, James, editor. *The International Standard Bible Encyclopedia.* Grand Rapids: Wm. B. Eerdmans Publishing Co., 1939.

Buttrick, George A., editor. *The Interpreter's Dictionary of the Bible.* Nashville: Abingdon Press, 1962.

Doughlas, J.D., editor. *The New Bible Dictionary.* Grand Rapids: Wm. B. Eerdmans Publishing Co., 1970.

Kittel, G., editor. *The Theological Dictionary of the New Testament.* Grand Rapids: Wm. B. Eerdmans Publishing Co., 1964.

Commentaries Most Frequently Consulted

Jewish commentaries:

Norman C. Gore, *Tzeenah U-Reenah: A Jewish Commentary on the Book of Exodus.*

U. Cassuto, *A Commentary on the Book of Exodus.*

S.R. Hirsch, *The Pentateuch:* Vol. II, *Exodus* (second edition).

General Commentaries:

Charles R. Eerdman, *The Book of Exodus: An exposition.*
F.B. Meyer, *Exodus: A Devotional Commentary.*
Dewey M. Beggle, *Moses, The Servant of Yahweh.*
James Plastaras, *The God of Exodus.*
Martin Noth, *Exodus: A Commentary.*
G. Henton Davies, *Exodus: Introduction and Commentary* (Torch Bible Commentaries).
R.S. Driver, *The Book of Exodus* (Cambridge Bible).
R.E. Clements, *Exodus* (The Cambridge Bible Commentary).
Robert Jamieson, *Exodus* (A Commentary Critical, Experimental and Practical, Vol. I).
Canon Cook, *Exodus* ("The Speaker's Bible," Vol. I).
Roy L. Honeycutt, *Exodus* (The Broadman Bible Commentary).
A.H. McNeile, *The Book of Exodus* (Westminster Commentaries).
George Rawlinson, *Exodus* (Ellicott's Commentary on the Whole Bible).
J. Coert Rylaarsdam and J. Edgar Park, *The Book of Exodus* (The Interpreter's Bible, Vol. I).